THE STORY OF
ST. PAUL'S LIFE AND LETTERS

THE STORY OF
ST. PAUL'S LIFE
AND LETTERS

BY
J. PATERSON SMYTH,
B.D., Litt.D., LL.D., D.C.L.

LONDON
SAMPSON LOW, MARSTON & CO., LTD.

MADE AND PRINTED IN GREAT BRITAIN BY
PURNELL AND SONS, PAULTON (SOMERSET) AND LONDON

CONTENTS

PART I
INTRODUCTORY

THE STORY OF
ST. PAUL'S LIFE AND LETTERS

———— ✦•✦•✦ ————

PART I
INTRODUCTORY

————

CHAPTER I

HOW TO STUDY ST. PAUL

ONE sometimes wonders why we should have in
the Bible so much more of the Life and Letters of the
one apostle whom Christ appointed after His Ascension than of the others whom He appointed in His
earthly life. But we have no doubt that if only one
was to be given that one should be St. Paul. For no
one of the others, not St. Peter, not even St. John,
counted for so much in the beginnings of the
Christian Church.

It is almost impossible to overstate what Paul meant
to Christianity. The simple, affectionate peasant men
of Galilee could tell with convincing power as no
others could, of the wonderful three years when they
walked with Jesus over the fields of Palestine, how
they learned to love Him as no man was ever loved

before, how they saw Him dead, how He came back to them alive, how their deep affection arose into wonder and awe and adoration as they realised who He was who was their Comrade and Friend. As one of themselves puts it long afterward * : "We declare to you that which we have heard, that which we have seen with our eyes, that which we beheld and our hands handled concerning the Word of Life. The Word became flesh and tabernacled among us and we beheld His glory, the glory as of the only begotten from the Father full of grace and truth." No one else could do what they did. The simple story, the deep conviction, the personal touch were irresistible.

But the Church had to go out into the Pagan world and down into the coming centuries, to meet cold indifference and clever scepticism and fierce opposition and controversies too keen for " unlearned and ignorant men." Was that why the Lord of the Church intervened, who had promised to be with it always to the end of the world ? He called to Him a man, gave him personal touch with Himself, convinced him beyond all gainsaying, won his passionate adoring gratitude and love—a man who was a genius, a scholar, a thinker and intellectual leader of men, and, above all, a man who, in his utter devotion all his life after, delights to call himself " the bond-slave of Jesus Christ." That is the marvellous thing in the story of Paul, who had never seen Jesus in the flesh and who was so obstinately unbelieving—the utter trust, the complete surrender, the close, reverent, personal love which the Lord won from him in that mysterious hour on the road to Damascus.

* John i. : 1 ; John i. : 14.

II

We are to study his life-story. It is not easy, for the beginning and end of the story are cut off. We have only the record of his middle life from the day when, in his mature manhood, St. Luke met him and began putting him into his diary, to the day, thirty years later, when the diarist dropped his pen, probably stricken from him by the hand of death. We have no record of his youth, no record of his old age, nor of the end. Though in another sense than his Lord, he seems to come to us like Melchisedek, " without father or mother or genealogy, without beginning of days or end of life."

And even that imperfect story is full of gaps. The biographer was not always present. There were many things that he did not know. Take for example this one sentence out of one of Paul's letters * : " Of the Jews five times received I forty stripes save one ; thrice was I beaten with rods ; once was I stoned ; thrice I suffered shipwreck, a night and a day I have been in the deep ; in perils of water, in perils of robbers, in perils among false brethren, in hunger and thirst, in fastings, in cold, in nakedness."

Not one of the five scourgings finds place in the history ; not one of the three shipwrecks, though a later one is described fully. No word of that terrible night and a day clinging probably to a raft in the wide Mediterranean. Think of all the romantic interest of the robber attacks in the mountains ; of the river suddenly rising in flood to sweep away the boats. What an interesting life of Paul we should have if we knew it all.

* 2 Cor. xi. : 24.

III

Happily, we are not quite left to St. Luke's diary. There are thirteen of St. Paul's letters bound up in the New Testament. Some others seem to have been lost, and unfortunately, we have so badly arranged those thirteen as to spoil their value in some degree to the general reader. There is no attempt at chronological order, no attempt, it would seem, at any order except that of placing them according to length, which not only confuses the sequence of facts mentioned in them, but also obscures the gradual development of the writer's thought and teaching. We have known all this for a long time but we are too conservative to alter it. Let us hope that some Bible publisher will some day put it right. In this book I have attempted to place the letters in their order, and, as far as possible, to put each in its right setting.

These letters illumine the whole story. They not only give us additional facts, but they do much towards giving us the man himself. For they are real letters, not formal treatises or sermons (except perhaps the Epistle to the Romans). Genuine letters to living men whom he knew and cared for, giving immediate answers to pressing questions and warnings and exhortations bearing on the everyday life of people with whom he was intimate—easy, natural letters like our own, giving the personal touch, the impetuous temper, the affectionate nature of the man.

Indeed, for our purpose they are rather better than our own letters, for they are dictated, and so come straight from his heart. Busy men then as now dictated their letters, and perhaps Paul's eyesight made it more necessary   So we read, *e.g.* : " I, Tertius,

who write this epistle, salute you." Then at the close
Paul scrawls in his ending : " I, Paul, salute you with
mine own hand, which is my token in every epistle."

The man just talked as he walked the room, or sat
on the floor working with the tent-cloth on his knees.
You can hear him talk, you can see him impetuously
break off in the middle of a sentence as a new thought
strikes him. It puzzles commentators, but it gives
you the living Paul.

IV

It is well worth while for any Bible reader to give
several months of his Bible-reading time to the careful,
deliberate study of St. Paul. Let him take a month,
if necessary, to one epistle. One book thoroughly
studied is worth a dozen superficially read, and each
book so studied will whet the desire and strengthen
the habit of studying other portions with similar care.*

Perhaps the reading of this present little volume
may help as a preliminary to such study. For further
help I offer a few suggestions :

In reading the history in the Acts of the Apostles
let imagination play on it, supplying form and colour,
living in the scene, making pictures. It is the main
secret of pleasurable reading, " Put yourself in his
place," not merely in picturing the outward scene but
also, in so far as may be, entering into the mind of
the speakers and actors. Anyone can do it and it is

* There is much to be said in favour of steady, systematic reading
according to a calendar by which the portion for each day is definitely
fixed. Yet as a rule one can seldom do very thorough study by that
way *alone*. Perhaps for some readers it would be well to combine
it with the method here recommended—to read, say, in the morning
according to the calendar, and at night to aim at the slower and more
thorough study of certain special books as suggested above,

worth the effort. True, a more vivid imagination will give one an advantage over another, but all that is really needful is some little knowledge of the circumstances and surroundings and the effort to think oneself into them.

To do this you must bring in the Epistles. You want to feel his mind, you want to read his letters, if you would know Paul. It is in letters to his friends that a man shews his heart.

When you have got the right setting for it, first read your Epistle rapidly straight through two or three times to get your grip of it as a whole. Then go over it in detail with a simple commentary (*e.g.*, The Cambridge Bible for Schools). Try to put yourself into the place of the writer and the readers. Do not read it as if addressed to you. He had no thought of you. He did not write for publication. He never imagined in his wildest dreams that he was writing scriptures for the Church for all the ages. True, the Holy Spirit was guiding him, but if you are to understand the letters of St. Paul you must take them quite naturally as letters written like your own, with no thought of anyone but the persons you are writing to.

Read the letters naturally. Get in sympathy with the writer. Feel with him in his rejoicing, in his despondency, in his exultant fighting moods, in his keen irony, in his sensitiveness when people have hurt him by ugly insinuations. Feel with him in his affectionate greetings, " God is my witness, how I long after you all," in his impetuous temper, where he is vexed with these " fools of Galatians," in his love for his fellow countrymen, " I would be willing to be accursed from Christ for the sake of my brethren."

Watch the little personal touches. He sends his love to Rufus and his mother, " who is also a mother to me," and you see the gratitude of a lonely man to a dear, kindly old lady who had mothered him. Watch him in Rome chained to a soldier as he writes the familiar ending to his epistle, " I, Paul, salute you with my own hand. Remember my chains." You can hear the fetters clanking as he tries to write. Or read that exquisite little note to Philemon, whose young slave had robbed him and run off to Rome to have a good time. Paul seems to have met the scamp and won him to religion and grown to love him dearly. Now he is sending him back with this note in his pocket. " Receive him," he says, " he is my child Onesimus, whom I have begotten in my bonds. I will repay that money. I might have demanded this favour of thee, for thou owest me thine own soul. But for love sake I only entreat it as Paul the aged prisoner of Jesus Christ."

I have been thinking chiefly here of the human side, of the human interest in the Bible, for the ignoring of it by religious people has tended much to make Bible reading uninteresting and unreal. Is it necessary here to remind any reader that the more he habituates himself to read his Bible naturally and sympathetically, recognising fully the human side of it, the more necessary it is to remember with reverence and awe that God is, in the truest sense, its author ; the more he enjoys the personality of the writers, the more needful to keep in mind that the writings " came not by the will of man, but holy men of God spake as they were moved by the Holy Ghost " ?

CHAPTER II

THE GREEK, THE ROMAN AND THE JEW

FULLY to understand Paul's life we need to understand Paul's world. We turn to secular history for the picture of his environment—the people amongst whom he moved. It helps us to appreciate his eagerness and the need and heart hunger of that lonely world.

Paul's world was the Roman Empire. Here are three great varieties of national life. The Greek, and the Roman, and the Jew divide the world between them. When Pilate wrote the inscription on the Cross in Hebrew, Greek and Latin, it was for them. It expresses the position as it appeared to Pilate—as it appeared to Paul—the three people, Hebrew, Greek and Roman. We shall afterwards see how wonderfully in God's providence they were combined to prepare for the coming of the Christ. The Jew, with his Bible and his religion, and his hope of the Messiah. The Greek, with his flexible language, the universal language of civilisation, making a vehicle for the gospel message. The Roman, welding together in the strong framework of the empire, the incoherent provinces and peoples on which Christianity was to act.

Keep these people steadily before you. Paul was always in the midst of them. Whether in Jerusalem, or Corinth, or Athens, or Rome, or in his boyhood home in Tarsus—everywhere was the Greek and the Roman and the Jew. It was to them he brought the story of the crucified Christ. He knew their need.

They, from their high position, looked down with contempt on him. But he, from his higher position, looked down with love and pity on them, for he knew that in its inner heart that poor world was tired and lonely, and that only Christ could help.

But we cannot discuss that here. I want you to see these people amongst whom Paul lived. I want to bring that old world before you.

II

There were the Greeks, the proud, eager, restless, beautiful Greeks, with their noble art and literature and philosophy, and their love of the beautiful, and their poetic imagination which peopled Olympus with the gods. To this day the whole civilised world looks to these ancient Greeks with wonder and gratitude. We owe to them the best of our culture. Above all things they stood for culture. Never was any nation prouder of its culture. Never had any nation better reason to be proud.

But, alas, we are learning in these days what culture can come to without religion, and the poor Greeks of St. Paul's day were learning what Germany may some day learn for her eternal good, that the world cannot get on with culture only. I picture these Greeks as like the modern Parisians, a light, pleasant, quick-witted people, who like to amuse themselves, to enjoy themselves. But the enjoyment was a good deal on the surface. Down underneath, life was a bit pathetic

Their best days were over. The golden age of Greece was in the past. Their political integrity was lost. They spent their time in frivolity, and worse. Profligacy and corruption were eating like a cancer, and their beautiful religion had no power to check their bad propensities. How could it? Even in the best days their beautiful gods on Mount Olympus were not very moral. You could not imagine anyone offering them spiritual prayers.

But at any rate, their gods were real to them then. They had some spiritual vision. They were men. Jove was the good-natured father and creator. Their gods fought with them at the Pass of Thermopylæ, where the famous 300 laid down their lives for Greece and for right.

But now they were a hopeless and effeminate race. Though they kept up their forms and their images, they had utterly lost all real belief. Their mythology had become a fairy tale. "Men had climbed up into Olympus and found no gods there." And so it was a lonely world. The Bishop of Tokyo told me the other day that this is the condition of Japan to-day. In young, happy days, nations and men can get on with frivolity and pleasure, and statues and poetry, but there are days when these things fail. In our sorrowful times we want a god of some kind to turn to. Even Jupiters and Junos will be some use provided we believe in them. But, alas, if we do not!

III

Then there were the Romans. The Roman Empire in Paul's day was in no decline like the Greek. The Romans were the masters of the world. It was a proud

boast even of Paul himself to be a Roman citizen—
a member of the great Roman Empire, with its wise
laws, its splendid armies, its boundless wealth, its
world-wide rule. Rome was the very personification
of pagan power and pride and mastery. That was her
imperial ambition. For that she kept her unconquer-
able armies ; for that she trampled weaker peoples into
the ground. The Roman was the German of those
ancient days in his pride of power and mastery and
success. The Roman was the super-man. His kingdom
was utterly a kingdom of this world. It was a
brave, splendid, magnificent world. You cannot help
admiring it.

But read the great historians and you see that underneath all the power and magnificence was a sink of
rottenness. Tourists are shown in Rome to-day the
splendid marble palaces of the emperors. Paul's
emperor, Nero, lived in one of these palaces. He was
outwardly a scholar and a polished gentleman. But
in his marble palace he executed his old mother and
kicked his wife to death, and in later days covered
Christians with tar and burned them for torches to
light the palace grounds.

Travellers to-day wonder at the Roman amphi-
theatres, the stupendous relics of national greatness.
The Coliseum held 30,000 spectators ; the Circus
Maximus held 200,000. But the historians teach us
that they were built on blood and agony by hosts of
wretched slaves. That when built they were crowded
daily with maddened, yelling multitudes of men,
women, and even children, citizens of Rome, watching
the horrible carnivals of blood. Under Trajan 10,000
gladiators were used up in a half year. Men fought

with lions and tigers. Serpents and crocodiles were brought to keep up the novelty. Women fought women, dwarfs fought dwarfs, blindfolded men fought each other, while the citizens cheered and laid bets on the fight. How could they be other than degraded and brutalised? You want to realise the position if you are to understand the terrible intensity of St. Paul with his gospel of Christ.

Slavery was the blackest curse to the empire. The invincible armies brought multitudes of captives from all over the world. Strong men, beautiful women, many of them refined, educated people, reduced to slavery. Two men out of every three who walked the streets of Rome were slaves. Aye, and two women out of every three, and two girls out of every three. Think of it. When every man could do what he liked with his slave. Every gust of passion, every suggestion of lust, the slaves must bear it. The slaves were wretched. The best of them crowded into Christianity for comfort. The worst of them debauched Rome. They brought in new, unnatural, abominable vices. They corrupted their masters. They corrupted the children. Every passion of the golden youth of Rome was ministered to by them. In the purlieus of the bath, and the circus, and the stage, the Roman boys learned what they should never have known. They grew old and jaded, and rotten with indulgence of vice before they were out of their teens. A world without God.

Yet they had gods in multitudes, in every street, in every home. If a man wanted money, or success in some evil scheme, he hired a priest and invoked the gods. But prayer had no moral significance. No man would think of unburdening his soul to his gods.

Then they wanted novelty in their religion. In Paul's day they had begun to introduce the oriental religions, with their shameless impurities, and the wild orgies of prostitution in the open temple, in the sight of the sun, before the altars of the Goddess of Fruitfulness. Here one dare not do more than hint at these abominations. I only hint at them at all that you may be helped to realise the awful need of Christ in that splendid, successful, godless world. How deeply Paul felt it is indicated in his terrible first chapter of the Epistle to the Romans "God gave men up to uncleanness through the lusts of their own hearts."

IV

The Greek, the Roman, and then the Jew. The mysterious, miraculous Jew. You can hardly doubt God's hand, and the providential preparation for Christ, when you see spread out over the empire the one race set apart from of old, with their genius for religion ; their worship of the one holy God ; their complete Old Testament as we have it to-day. They were everywhere. From distant Babylon, the land of Shadrach, Meshach and Abednego, to all the coasts around the Mediterranean. You remember the list of them that came back to the Pentecost—" Parthians and Medes and Elamites, and dwellers in Mesopotamia, in Pontus and Asia, in Phrygia and Pamphylia, in Egypt and Libya," etc. Think what it meant in that poor unholy world, with its multitude of degrading gods, to have in every city the worship of the one God, holy and pure ; men with the spiritual vision of sin and righteousness ; men with the inspired Bible in their hands ; men with the eager outlook for a golden age in the future when Messiah should come to bless the people of God.

True, they were a narrow and bigoted people ; true, when Messiah came they crucified Him ; true, they were the bitter enemies of the Church which set out to preach that crucified Messiah. But you can see how their presence all over the empire laid a broad foundation for Christianity to build on. And in one of their Jewish homes in the city of Tarsus they were rearing up a boy named Saul.

PART II
YOUTH AND PREPARATION TIME

PART II

YOUTH AND PREPARATION TIME

CHAPTER III

THE THOUGHTS OF YOUTH ARE LONG, LONG THOUGHTS

UNEXPECTEDLY, suddenly, out of the unknown, Saul of Tarsus makes his first appearance on the stage of history. The curtain rises on a howling Eastern mob and stones hurtling through the air, and a young Jewish rabbi in the background with white robes piled at his feet. Amid this crowd of 'cursing fanatics gnashing with their teeth," they stoned Stephen calling upon God, and the witnesses laid down their clothes at a young man's feet whose name was Saul."

This is our first sight of Saul of Tarsus. He is here called a young man, but he is already prominent in Jerusalem, so we may set him down as probably about thirty years of age. We have no earlier knowledge of him except from a few hints in his letters and speeches, but we can gather something from them.

I

We can go back twenty years. When the boy Jesus was playing in the carpenter's shop, and the boy John, his forerunner, was growing up in the hill country of Judea, away across the sea in the pagan city of Tarsus, was another boy who in human sight had no connection with either, but who learned in later years that God had destined him from his mother's womb* to stand beside them both in the eternal purpose of humanity.

The memories of childhood are the most lasting of all. I want you to see the " pictures that hung upon Memories wall " when Paul thought of his boyhood. Tarsus was a town rather like Montreal in its earlier days, a University town and a great central mart of trade, especially the lumber trade. You could see the barefoot loggers riding on the logs and prizing open the jam above the Cydnus Falls. It was in a fine position for commerce. Behind it through the mountains ran the " Cilician gates," the traders' mountain pass to the lands beyond the Taurus. Through the midst of the town the navigable river Cydnus ran down to the sea, with its crowded ships, and quays, and dockyards. Saul's grandfather saw the mountain as a robber's fastness, and the river as a shelter for the pirates of the Levant. When Saul's father was a boy (B.C. 41), all Tarsus crowded on the river's bank to see the gorgeous pageant that day when Cleopatra sailed up the Cydnus attired as Venus in her golden barge to meet Mark Antony. I am not sure whether the banquet was at Tarsus or Alexandria when she dissolved her pearls in the wine, but at any rate

* Gal. 1. : 15.

the old Pharisee would not have been invited there
So you see Tarsus was not without its romantic stories.

There I see the boy Saul watching the ships with
his companions ; shouting to the lumbermen floating
past ; climbing on the bales of goods piled along the
quay ; listening to the traders, in their varied costumes
and varied dialects, from all parts of the empire.   And
the lad evidently took notice, for long afterwards in
his letters we find the illustrations of the sealing, and
the earnest money, and the branding of bales, and the
hucksterings, and the adulterations of goods.   And I
note that in the providence of God the man who was to
spend his life in pagan cities was brought up in a pagan
city.   He who was to preach a universal religion for all
races was brought up, not on the green hills of Galilee,
but in a crowded centre of trade where all races met.

II

He was proud of his native town.   " It was no mean
city," he says.   And he was proud of his ancestry.
The Roman boy might look down on the Jewish boy,
but the Jewish boy knew he belonged to a race that
was making history before Rome was born.   He belonged to the famous little tribe of Benjamin, and was
namesake of the famous Benjamite, King Saul.   When
the other Tarsus boys played soldiers in the woods, or
dreamed, as boys do, of old heroic days—of the fight
at Marathon—of Romulus and Remus—and

> " How Horatius kept the bridge
> In the brave days of old,"

Saul fed his imagination on Abram and Jacob, and the
brilliant adventures of Joseph in Egypt—on Elijah

and Saul and David and Daniel and Shadrach, Meshach and Abednego, and the wild days, dear to a boyish mind, when Samson was smashing the Philistines' skulls with an ass's jawbone. That is the sort of thing that appeals to a boy.

And when the other boys learned of Jupiter and Juno and Venus, Saul learned of the Almighty, all-holy Jehovah, the God of his own people.

III

His father in that business town was probably a merchant. He was evidently a man of some position (the fact that his son was a tent-maker proves nothing against this. Every Jewish boy learned a trade). He had won the proud distinction of citizenship of Rome. Paul says he was a Hebrew of the Hebrews, a Pharisee of the Pharisees, of the strictest sect of his religion. You can see him walking, in his broad phylacteries, strict in ritual observances. I think of him as an austere man, a righteous man, silent, strict, bigoted, like the old Scotch covenanters. I wonder if he was in St. Paul's mind when he wrote " Fathers provoke not your children to wrath." I should not wonder if he did not spare the rod on young Saul. I should not wonder if young Saul needed the rod, judging from Saul, the fierce, passionate persecutor, and even from the Paul of later life, though chastened and softened by the grace of God. I can well imagine that his father found him a passionate strong-willed boy, not very easy to bring up, and I can well believe that in later days, heart-broken by that son's apostacy, when he disgraced the proud old name and became a renegade from the faith, that that father could choke down his love and disown his son, and turn him out penniless to follow the sect of the Nazarenes. Perhaps that was why he was so poor all his days, and so sensitively proud that he would not allow his people to help him.

We learn that Saul had a sister, who was afterwards married in Jerusalem, and some cousins or kinsmen, who, he says, " were in Christ before me."* I wish we knew something of his mother. One always wants to know what the mothers of great men were like. He never mentions her. Perhaps her husband made her cast him off when he disgraced the family. Perhaps she died early. Somehow, I always think of him as a motherless boy. Perhaps that accounts for the touching little reference in the close of one of his letters : " Salute Rufus and his mother, who was also a mother to me."† That kindly old lady who took his mother's place for him.

IV

Whether we are right or not in guessing his father to be a Tarsus business man, at any rate he seemed to have designed his son for the ministry—what the modern business man does not. I wonder why ? You are not mere money-seekers. Many of you are good Christian people. And with splendid self-sacrifice you gave your boys to the war. Why do you not give your boys a chance of finding their vocations to the noblest of all professions—and the happiest ? In all sincerity I say to you to-day—with all its difficulties,

* Rom. xvi. : 7.   † Rom. xvi.: 13.

and strain and worry—I would not change my office for that of a king on his throne. If I had a dozen boys I would wish them all as I am. Of course, you cannot decide for them, but you could give them a chance to decide. Does no mother dream the dream for her boy of helping the tempted and preaching God's fatherhood, and consecrating at the altar the bread from heaven for the strengthening of human souls? Let us hope in this new, solemn world after the war, when our boys come home, we shall have a better story to tell.

V

So one day Saul went off to Jerusalem to college A great day to a Hebrew boy when he first sees the holy city—the dream city of his people. And a great day when he first goes to college, and greater still when, as he tells us, the president of the college is the famous Rabbi Gamaliel, a doctor of the law, " held in honour of all the people." His fame is not confined to the Christian New Testament. The Jewish Talmud has embalmed his memory. Every educated Jew in this land to-day can tell you of Gamaliel's place in history. Not only a famous scholar, but a broad, large-minded leader of thought. So says the Jewish Talmud. So says the Christian New Testament. Take that one instance in the Acts of the Apostles, when his bigoted fellow priests were persecuting the Christians, " Let them alone," said Gamaliel, " if this thing be of men it will come to naught, but if it be of God, ye cannot overthrow it, lest haply ye be found even to fight against God."* A broad-minded man.

* Acts v.: **39**.

One wonders why Christianity did not appeal to him. But it did not. There is a legend that it did, but I do not believe it. The Jews know nothing of it. He lived and died a Jew, and before he died he wrote a long liturgical prayer against this new heresy of the Nazarenes.

You can see what an advantage it was to the impetuous Saul to be under the influence of that wise, calm leader all his college years. Saul did well in college. " I advanced," he says, " beyond many of my age in learning the Jews' religion."

The teaching in those days was more interesting than the college lectures of our day—more conversational. The students were accustomed and encouraged to ask questions all through the teaching. Our Professors require silence in the class-room. The students in Saul's days " sat at the feet of the doctors hearing them and asking questions."

Does not that start in your memory some words of St. Luke about the boy Jesus ? Did you ever think of Jesus at Gamaliel's lectures. I may be wrong, but I cannot help thinking what happened one day in Jerusalem—of a boy twelve years old getting lost for three days, while his frightened people searched everywhere for him. I think of that lost boy, wandering all over the strange city, sleeping where he could at night, getting food from some kind woman in the daytime, and at last on the third day wandering into Gamaliel's class-rooms in the Temple precincts and sitting down with the other students. And there the distracted mother finds him " in the midst of the doctors, hearing them and asking them questions."* Is not that what

* Luke ii. : 46.

you would expect of Jesus? Not a boy pertly examining the great rabbis, but a modest pupil learning at their feet.

Of course it is a conjecture, but I think it quite probable that one day Jesus sat like Saul at the feet of Gamaliel.

VI

Paul says of his studies—" I advanced beyond many of my age." What were his studies? The Bible. The Bible only.

Spoiled, no doubt, by stupid rabbinical commentary, as it is spoiled to-day by our stupid clerical sermons. But you cannot quite spoil the Bible. Saul knew it as you know your alphabet. He knew it in Hebrew and Septuagint Greek—as we see from his quotations—and he knew it by heart. He could not carry bulky rolls around with him. His speeches in the Acts contain quotations and allusions from nearly every Old Testament book. In his epistles are 198 quotations. The man's mind was saturated with scripture. Who doubts that it told largely in making him the great man he was? No wonder he thought it the world's great treasure. " What advantage, then, hath the Jew?" he asks ; " chiefly that unto them were committed the oracles of God."

We have that Bible of his, and the New Testament with it, but our tables are strewn with light magazines, and the newsboy piles up on our doorstep the *Gazette*, and the *Star*, and the *Herald*, and the *Evening News*, and some of us have not time for anything higher. I do not want to scold about the Bible—I am not so good about it myself—but don't you think we might do better ? If the Scriptures are the power of God unto salvation, a storehouse of power from God, might we not at the least read a chapter before our prayers every night ? I hope most of us do. If anyone does not, will he resolve to begin now, taking one of the gospels to commence with ?

VII

We take a long step forward. Ten years have elapsed since Saul of Tarsus bade good-bye to his college and his wise old president, when we find him back in Jerusalem again. I think of him going to the school to greet his old master. In these ten years occurred the mission of Jesus and His crucifixion. Jerusalem is being deeply agitated by his followers, who claim that he is the Messiah ; that he is risen from the dead ; that he is the eternal Son of God. At first they were frightened and lay low, but after the first Pentecost, and the miracle of the Holy Spirit, they could no longer be held down. This glorious thing that they knew could no longer be kept to themselves. In the very streets of the city which had crucified him, they proclaimed Jesus and the Resurrection. Peter, a few weeks after his cowardly denial, flung his challenge in the teeth of priest and Pharisee. " Ye killed the Holy One and the Just, and desired a murderer to be granted unto you. Ye killed the Prince of Life whom God raised from the dead, of which we all are witnesses." And the people listened ; Jerusalem was deeply stirred.

At this crisis, as I judge, Saul came back to the capital. How do I know he had been away ? Well,

I cannot believe he was there during the ministry of Jesus, partly because he never hints of having seen Him on earth, partly because I judge that a man of Saul's type coming in personal contact with the Lord, must, perforce, either have persecuted Him or followed Him—and he certainly did neither.

Probably he left college for some country charge, as many of our students do, and just as the ablest of our young country clergy to-day are drawn back into the city, so the clever young rabbi soon gravitated to Jerusalem.

He came back with his splendid Jewish gospel that " God so loved—*the Jew*," that he chose him out of all the world to bless him, and one day would send the anointed Messiah to deliver Israel from the Roman power and raise it to a pinnacle of glory and righteousness. A brave, stirring gospel for the Jew.

But heretics in Jerusalem were teaching the Gospel of the Nazarene, and, worst still, they were being listened to. " The number of the disciples multiplied greatly, and a great company of priests were obedient to the faith."

" We are Jews," said these Nazarenes. " We believe in the Messiah, but there is no Messiah to look forward to now. The Messiah has come already, and you in your blind bigotry have crucified Him. But God has raised Him from the dead. Repent and receive Him everyone of you, and turn to God for forgiveness." That was not pleasant hearing for the Pharisees and scribes.

VIII

The worst of these heretics was Stephen, the deacon. He was afraid of no man. He challenged them all. They held a great debate one day in which the synagogue of the Cilicians took part. Paul was of Tarsus in Cilicia, and probably was in the debate. He was a clever debater, but in Stephen he found an adversary worthy of his steel. If Stephen had lived he might have been another Paul. Stephen was too strong for them in the debate. " They were not able to resist the wisdom and the spirit in which he spake." And soon after the whole city writhed under his public rebuke: " Ye stiff-necked and uncircumcised in heart and ears, ye do always resist the Holy Ghost. No wonder you persecuted and killed the Christ. Which of the prophets have not your fathers persecuted ? They showed you the coming of the righteous One, of whom now ye have been the betrayers and murderers " Certainly Stephen did not fight with kid gloves.

Saul and his party could stand no more. They must fight for the Faith. Stephen must die Be quite fair to them. They looked for a Messiah in power and glory who should make Israel and the faith of Jehovah triumphant in the earth. They believed that their holy religion was in danger. That it was blasphemy to worship a crucified Jew. Is it not written in the law " cursed is everyone who is hanged on a tree " ?

Men are quite right to fight for what they believe to be the truth, but these fought with the bigot temper, and the bigot slander, and the bigot misrepresenting of the other man's words. Just as in religious

controversies to-day, when Protestants and Roman
Catholics, churchmen and non-churchmen say unkind
things each about the other. By all means have controversy when truth is in danger. Without it
Christianity would have been swamped long ago, but let
it be Christian controversy—kindlyand honourable controversy, looking for truth and not for victory, thinking
and believing the best about opponents, never using
unfair arguments, never misrepresenting other men's
views, never maligning the motives of those who differ.
Say, we are on both sides honest men seeking the truth.
Let us listen to each other and trust each other.

Such controversy can do nothing but good, but it
was too much to expect in those old days. " So they
stoned Stephen, calling upon God and praying, ' Lord
Jesus receive my spirit. Lord, lay not this sin to their
charge.' And the witnesses laid down their clothes
at a young man's feet whose name was Saul."

IX

Saul never forgot that day. All through his life
you can see the keen remorse, " When the blood of thy
martyr Stephen was shed, I was standing by and con-
senting to his death. I am not worthy to be called
an Apostle because I persecuted the Church of God."

Looking back on it from his later years he would
probably see this day as one of the moulding influences
of his life. I wish he had told us how he felt that
night when the heretic was dead. Was conscience
stirring ? Was remorse beginning ? He was a brave
man himself and had seen a brave man die. He could
not easily forget that dying prayer. I wonder if Saul

lay awake that night—if he thought about what was happening outside in the darkness where devout men carried Stephen to his burial, and frightened women sobbed over a mangled corpse, " whose dead face was as it were the face of an angel."

Let me close with a lesson. Trust God when things are hopeless. God buries His workers, but carries on His work. On the first Good Friday Christ was dead. His enemies had triumphed. The hopes of the disciples seemed shattered for ever. But Easter came.

Now Stephen is dead, the ablest of their champions The chief hope of Christianity seemed dead with him. But truth cannot die. God is behind it. Who would have thought as Stephen fell that within a month his fiercest opponent would take his place and accomplish what Stephen could never have done ?

St. Augustine says in a sermon " that we owe Paul to the prayer of Stephen " : " *Si Stephanus non orasset Ecclesia Paulum non haberet.*" Truly God moves in a mysterious way His wonders to perform

CHAPTER IV

THE CRISIS OF CONVERSION

OUR last picture was the stoning of Stephen. We saw Saul looking down on a mangled corpse whose dead face was " as the face of an angel." I ventured to suggest that from what we know of his tenderness of heart in later life that already there would be in him the stirrings of pity and remorse. I still think the same, in spite of all the evidence against it. The more I know of him the more I think it.

But if it were so, he certainly gave no outward sign. He was " exceedingly mad " against the new religion. He made himself chief of the inquisition. Like Torquemada in Spain, like Claverhouse on the hills of Scotland, he harried the disciples from house to house, " and haling men and women committed them to prison."

Think of his inquisitors visiting houses in the night, dragging people out of their beds, and scourging not only men, but women. He mentions women three times as if in aggravation of his cruelty. Think of flogging a woman. The civilised world which took so calmly the killing of countless men in the War days were roused into fierce anger whenever women were ill-treated. Saul flogged women. He compelled the disciples to blaspheme the name of Jesus, and if they refused, he voted death for them. He tells us that himself. Stephen was not the only one stoned by him. He was the terror of the whole countryside He was cordially detested as well as feared. Far off as Damascus they know his evil fame—" how much evil he hath done. to thy saints at Jerusalem " ; how he hath made havoc of the Church, *i.e.*, rooted it up, as a wild boar would root up a garden. He was an obstinate, cruel man. Evidently he had not profited much by the wise, calm teaching of his old master Gamaliel.

Ah, poor Saul ! He was laying up bitter memories for himself in later days. He never got over the pain of it. Even in his old age, when he knew himself forgiven by God, he could never forgive himself. He had to go through it all himself later on. He was hated, and persecuted, and scourged and stoned. He never whines. I think it was rather a comfort to him that he should suffer what he had himself inflicted. At any rate, he takes it like a man—" rejoicing in tribulation. Our light affliction which is but for a moment." Saul was a very cruel man, but there was nothing small about him.

Naturally the disciples fled for their lives. All except the apostles, the appointed heads of the Church. Jerusalem was emptied of disciples ; no more street preaching ; no more meetings in the upper room. Saul had wiped out the plague from the Holy City. But with bitter anger he found that he had only spread it. " They that were scattered abroad went everywhere preaching the word." It was the first missionary triumph of the little Church. God thus overrules the designs of men.

II

Six months later I find Saul one morning with his company riding out of Jerusalem by the Damascus gate " breathing out threatenings and slaughter." He has 150 miles before him on a most interesting road, if his evil temper would let him think of it. Exquisite scenery alive with historic memories ; back to Naaman, the leper, back 2,000 years to Abram's old steward, Eleazar of Damascus.

But he was in no mood for scenery. He never did care for scenery any way. Not like Our Lord, who was a lover of nature, who talks of the lilies how they grow, and the red sunset sky, and the fowls of the air, and the fields white with the harvest.

Saul was a man of cities. You find no references to nature in his writings. And just now, especially, he has something else to think about. He is baffled and angry. A Christian conventicle has been set up in Damascus and Saul is out hunting for disciples.

Aye, but he is not the only hunter out this morning, for the Lord of the disciples is out hunting Saul. Do you know Thomson's famous poem, " The Hound of Heaven," telling of God's untiring, unceasing pursuit of the souls who are fleeing from Him ? He is always pursuing. Men call it doubt, misgivings, remorse, stirring of conscience. Men tell me sometimes how they lay awake all night, and their thoughts were hell to them. Do you ever feel like that—regrets and misgivings, remorse about your life ? That means God pursuing. It is the " Hound of Heaven " ever after you. It is the Good Shepherd on the desolate mountains, seeking what is lost if so be that he may find it. Think solemnly about it.

> For the Christ pursues as we rush on,
> With a sorrowful fall in his pleading tone :
> " Thou wilt tire in the dreary ways of sin,
> I left My home to bring thee in.
> In its golden street are no weary feet,
> Its rest is pleasant, its songs are sweet."
> And we shout back angrily, hurrying on
> To a terrible home where rest is none :
> " We want not your city's golden street,
> Nor to hear its constant song."
> *And still Christ keeps pursuing us, pursuing*
> *all along.*

And as He pursues us, so He pursued Saul. And it was harder for Saul to escape in those six days. For now he is out of the whirl and rush of life through which so many escape God. He has no one to talk to but his attendants. He has six days to ride alone. He has six nights to think.

He has been thinking at odd times lately, but had shaken off his thoughts. Now that he is alone the ghosts are coming back. In the secret tribunal of conscience he has to stand before himself. I feel that I am right that conscience was goading him. Jesus on the Damascus road knew what was in his heart. " It is hard for thee to kick against the goads." God knows what he is thinking—what secret misgivings, what haunting doubts come back : " Am I right in killing men and flogging women for their faith ? Could there be any doubt Stephen was wrong ? After all, Isaiah did write of a suffering Messiah, ' who hath borne our griefs and carried our sorrows, yet we did esteem him stricken smitten of God and afflicted.' But surely all my life study cannot be wrong. Gamaliel and all the clergy cannot be wrong. These are but temptations of the devil. To worship that crucified Nazarene is blasphemy against God, and I am determined to stamp it out. It is my duty to stamp it out."

He had reached the hilltop looking over Damascus. Then—in a moment—the crisis came. Suddenly from the heavens flashed a blinding glory, " above the brightness of the sun," he says ; " shining about me and them that travelled with me." And in the midst of the glory he saw—the Christ of God—whom he never again lost sight of all his life long. And a voice spake to him in the Hebrew tongue—a voice which he never ceased hearing all his life long. " Shaoul, Shaoul, why persecutest thou Me ? " " Who art thou, Lord ?" " I am Jesus whom thou persecutest." And he believed it, believed it instantly. No question, no doubt was possible to him then or for ever. Trembling and astonished he fell to the ground in absolute surrender. " Lord, what wilt thou have me do ? "

III

That is the story of the conversion of Saul. Explain it as you will ; think of it as you will. Saul was the only one who knew what happened. As to what he saw and heard he never wavered. He tells it repeatedly, and always substantially the same story. The men told it differently, confusedly. " They saw the glory. They stood speechless, hearing a voice, but seeing no one." That is what we should expect. It was not meant for them. It was meant for him. He knew It was the unalterable conviction of his life. It shook him to the depths of his innermost being. He had actually seen Jesus Christ.

The Hunter of Heaven had got him at last, and all life was changed. In an instant, as he fell there shattered and blinded by the roadside, he became Christ's man utterly and entirely for ever and ever.

Does anyone want to argue about it ? You have a perfect right to do so, but there is no basis for argument Nobody in the world knows anything about it except Paul. Paul was absolutely certain that he had seen the risen Lord. On that certainty he anchored all his hopes for time and eternity. All his life long he insists, " I know—not from men, or through men— but from Jesus Christ."

That is what gets me—that absolutely unshakeable conviction of the man himself. It was no vision, no dream, no hallucination of a disordered fancy. I have read the books that explain it away as the dream of an hysterical weakling. Paul was no hysterical weakling. If ever a man had a sane, healthy mind, Paul had. If ever a man felt sure of anything all through his life, Paul felt sure. If ever a man proved his belief by the sacrifice of his whole life, Paul proved it.

" I have seen the Lord." All his life he reiterated that, " I have seen Jesus Christ." It was not books, nor arguments, nor evidence of apostles. It was the actual appearance of the Risen Lord that made him a Christian ; that gave him boundless joy and certainty ; that gave him the Gospel of the Resurrection to preach. That is what gave Paul's preaching its tremendous reality. That is the difference between his preaching and ours. Only yesterday I thought as I meditated on the scene that, if Jesus appeared to me as He appeared to St. Paul, I would make you spring to your feet and follow Him to a man.

That was his claim to be as good an Apostle as the others : " Have I not seen Jesus Our Lord ! " When he is telling what the apostles told him of the appearances of Jesus after his resurrection—to Peter—to John—to 500 brethren, " Last of all He was seen of me also, as of one born out of due time," he puts the appearance to himself on an absolute par with the others.

And here is a point hardly ever noticed. When in his grand Resurrection chapter he speaks of the glorified spiritual body that shall be, where did he get his idea of the spiritual body ? You feel at once the picture in his mind. Where else could he have got the idea— the glorified Jesus as he saw him at Damascus, " who shall change our vile body that it may be like unto His glorious body "—that body which I saw that day at the Damascus gate.

IV

As one of the evidences of the truth of Christianity, do you see the tremendous force of this conversion of Paul ? That the determined enemy of Christianity should, in one hour, be so utterly changed into an un- shakeable believer, and a devoted lover of the Lord Jesus Christ, and joyfully sacrifice his whole life to his service. Unbelievers in our days may say that it is not easy to estimate the evidence for the story of Jesus who lived 2,000 years ago. But this Saul of Tarsus lived in Jesus' time. He was a very clever man. The evidence pro and con was ready to his hand. The living men were there to question. He knew all the

reasons that convinced Annas and Caiaphas that the
whole thing was an imposture. His whole brilliant
career was at stake. He had everything to lose ; he
had nothing to gain. He was absolutely prejudiced,
the whole attitude of his mind was dead against believing. Yet, in a moment—account for it as you may
—he had become Christ's man for ever. If Saul of
Tarsus was mistaken that day, I can only say that it
was one of the most improbable and incomprehensible
mistakes in the whole of history.

v

Now I see the attendants lift from the road a broken,
trembling man, with shattered nerves and eyes blinded
by the shock, as they lead him by the hand into Damascus. He refuses food ; he refuses greetings. He only
wants to get away from everybody—to be alone. For
three terrible days and nights he was alone in a dark
room, and neither did eat nor drink—alone with
his conscience, alone with his God—thinking, thinking.
When a great soul is being torn up by the roots the
crisis can only come thus in agony and shame.

No one can ever tell what passed through his soul
in these three silent days, but one thought there must
have been, to still the agony of remorse—the thought
of the tender, forgiving love of Christ who had come
to him. That He should come after the Resurrection
to His beloved disciples in Galilee was to be expected,
but that He should come to him and forgive and bless,
and receive a wicked torturer and slaughterer and
persecutor ! Ah, Saul never could forget that. We
have seen how he never forgot his wickedness of

the past. But it was because he never forgot either
the tender kindness of Jesus.

To every true man that is what most deepens
the sorrow for sin. That the Lord whom he has
ill-treated should love him and forgive him. Ah,
it is worth while loving that way. It pays. Christ
gets great results. Saul became His follower and lover,
and devoted slave all the days of his life. The love
of Christ is the very centre of his gospel.

With that joy in his heart you cannot entirely
pity Saul in his terrible struggle. Soon the peace
of God came stealing into his heart, and the crisis
ended with a sobbing man on his knees. And the
Lord saw him, and the message came to Ananias in
a dream : " Go down Straight Street, and enquire
for Saul of Tarsus, for, behold, he prayeth." Did you
ever think of God knowing your street and number
of your house ? " Go down to such a street and enquire
for A.B., for behold he prayeth ! "

VI

The next words in the history rather jar on me.
Immediately, says St. Luke, he began to preach
Jesus that He is the Son of God. Somehow that
does not seem like the Saul that we know. I can
quite see that it would make a great sensation and
draw much attention to the Gospel of Christ. And
I can quite believe that after a sudden change the
really converted drunkard, and the really converted
prize-fighter, that we sometimes hear of, might make
Christ more real than some of our clergy could make

Him, but this does not quite fit in with what we know of the great souls, the deep, earnest spirits, who, after a sudden conversion, have influenced the world. They need a breathing space. They need to learn— to co-ordinate their troubled thoughts. They need to think and meditate, and still the tumults of their emotions, and commune in secrecy and silence with their souls and with God.

A reserved man does not talk about these secret things of life. Probably Luke never knew. The only hint we have is one single verse in the letter to the Galatians : " After it pleased God to reveal His Son in me, immediately I conferred not with flesh and blood, but I went into Arabia, and returned again unto Damascus." That is all.

You see, St. Luke's story is all right about the preaching in Damascus, but he does not know, or at any rate does not tell, about this retirement to Arabia. We do not know either, except those few words, but, at least it leaves room for the conjecture that pictures the lonely man for months in the deserts of Arabia, in the shadow of Mount Sinai, thinking, brooding, meditating, restudying his Bible in the new light come to him—planning his future in the service of his dear Lord—and, above all, praying, living in communion with God. That is what makes big men. That is what makes great preachers. It would make a vast difference in the preaching of Christ's gospel if we clergy spent more time in communion with God. Brethren, pray for us.

VII

Suddenly, one day this grave, solemn man reappeared in the city, and at once began his daring mission, and " confounded the Jews who dwelt in Damascus, proving that this is the very Christ."

But the Jews would not listen to him. They hated him as a renegade. They watched the gates day and night to kill him, and at length the disciples one night planned his escape, and lowered him over the wall in a basket.

So his first attempt was a bad failure. But you could not discourage a man who felt God behind him. " I'll make men listen yet," said Disraeli, when he failed in his first speech in the House of Commons. " I'll make them listen yet," said Paul, when they hunted him from Damascus. So he took his next step. He would very much like to go back to Jerusalem to see the divinely appointed heads of the Church, and especially he wanted to see Peter their chief.

So, friendless and penniless, he started to walk that long one hundred and fifty miles. We are told nothing of that journey. But you know without any telling that the lonely man knelt down in the darkness as he passed the spot where Christ appeared to him. You know how he must have felt as he passed the scene of Stephen's murder. You can feel with him as he passed the old college walls in Jerusalem, knowing that his old master and his old friends would never speak to him again—a renegade from their holy faith.

However, it would be all right, he thought, when he saw the disciples. But the disciples did not want to see him. They were afraid of him. They did not trust him. It took all the persuasion of his old friend Barnabas even to get him an interview with Peter and James.

VIII

For fifteen days he stayed there in intercourse with Peter. The Bible is a very tantalising book. It says no word of these fifteen days. What a dramatic picture that intercourse would make. The two great leaders of the Church—two honest, earnest, loving men —Saul listening, Peter telling the story of the three wonderful years with Jesus.

I hear Saul impetuously breaking in with questions. I fancy him one night opening his heart : " Peter, what I feel most is the wonder of His love. That He should love and forgive a murderer, a blasphemer, a persecutor." And Peter replies : " Saul, it was just like Him. He was always like that. You don't know my story. I was a worse man than you. You were not a coward, anyway. He picked me out of all the world to be His closest friend, and the night before they killed Him I turned against Him and denied Him while He lay helpless in His enemies' hands. I cursed and swore that I never knew Him. He just raised His eyes as He heard, and the sorrow in that look nearly broke my heart. I rushed out and wept bitterly. I walked the streets all night. I would have given anything to go back and tell Him how sorry I was, but I had no chance Next day they crucified Him. It was too late then.

For three black, awful days I slunk away in my shame and misery. The Master who loved me was lying cold and dead in Joseph's tomb, and the last words He had heard from me were words of blasphemous denial. Oh, if He could only know how sorry I was! Then the Easter morning came. The Lord was risen. And what do you think? I found He had known and was thinking of me those three days in the World of the Departed. I found He had left a message with the angels at the tomb. ' Go tell my disciples, and especially tell Peter.' Tell Peter! Tell me! Could I ever forget that? I, who had been a traitor, an apostate, I, who did not think myself a disciple any more? Tell Peter! Do you wonder that I love Him? Do you wonder that I would die for Him? "

CHAPTER V

Saul of Tarsus Finds His Life Work

Paul, on that interesting fortnight's visit, did not spend all his time with Peter. He went out through the city. He tried to preach. He could not keep to himself the great discovery. He thought that what so convinced him must convince everybody. But he failed badly. Nobody would listen to him. Every speech was a signal for a riot. Every sentence was punctuated with curses and stones. It was a worse failure even than that in Damascus.

He felt it keenly. He tells us later that he went to the temple and on his knees told his troubles to God. "Lord, nobody will listen to me. They know too much about me; that I imprisoned and flogged in every synagogue, and when the blood of thy Martyr Stephen was shed I held the raiment of them that slew him."

He saw he had failed. I daresay Peter and Barnabas had already told him, "Saul, it is no use, you are only making trouble." At last, when his life was endangered, the disciples brought him down to Cæsarea—where so many of the shipping lines called—and thence he sailed to Tarsus.*

I wonder why? If there was any reason to think that his family had become Christian or friendly I

* Acts ix. : 30.

should think it quite natural that a tired, broken man would want to go home and let his mother comfort him, and rest him till his nerves grew quieted and he could start again. There is no one like the dear old mother at such a time. But there is no justification for supposing that there were any of his family or friends to greet him. Saul had to remain a lonely man all his life. He had the Lord Jesus for his friend and that must suffice him.

> Without the cheer of sister or of daughter,
> Without the stay of father or of son,
> Lone on the land and homeless on the water,
> Passed he in patience till his work was done.

A well-known writer suggests that one of his three shipwrecks might have occurred on this voyage, and landed him, without his will, in the harbour of his native town. We do not know. At any rate he need not have stayed there. But he did.

Twenty years ago he had left Tarsus to go to college. It was a lonely thing to come back after twenty years to the boyhood home. In twenty years people die ; people grow old and forget—and if you come back with the stigma of renegade and with the stigma of failure when you are approaching forty, they forget still more. New faces met him in the old haunts. A new generation of boys tramped on the wharf and shouted to the lumbermen on the river as he had done twenty years before.

It was lonely. It made a man feel old. Probably he tried to preach—and probably he failed. The proverb about the prophet in his own country is all the stronger when that prophet is not liked. It was a trying time, but it was God's training for him. All study of famous biographies teaches that God trains his greatest servants largely by times of depression, and loneliness, and failure, and disappointment.

There we leave him for the present, thinking, brooding, forgotten of men, eating out his heart in his boyhood's home, wondering if those sins of his past life would forever prevent success in preaching about his Lord.

II

Again the scene changes. And Saul is not in the new scene. It is a city, the magnificent heathen city of Antioch in Syria. Paul's story will always take us to cities and crowds. Already Tarsus, Jerusalem, Damascus, now a city greater still and more important in the history of Paul and of the early Church. After Jerusalem, Antioch became the second mother of the Church. Antioch became the centre of Gentile Christianity. Antioch became the central home of Paul for twenty years. " And the disciples were called Christians first in Antioch."

Since Antioch bulks so largely in our story we had better try to visualise it, that we may remember it each time we come to it. First from the outside. Call up in your minds the North-east angle of the Mediterranean, the shores of Palestine forming one side and the shores of Asia Minor meeting it at right angles. There is Antioch on the river Orontes, in touch with all places, an ideal centre for a Church which was to spread among the Gentiles. Whenever Paul saw from his ship that angle of the coast it meant home. Then, landing at the Antioch port, Seleucia, he passed up through groves of palm and olive and myrtle, and gardens bright with gorgeous flowers, into the city of palaces, the queen of the East, the third metropolis of the world—the nearest approach to home that Paul ever had.

You cannot visualise a whole city. When I think of Montreal I picture its main artery, St. Catherine Street, four miles long, with Mount Royal on the north, dominating all. When an Antioch man thought of Antioch he thought of its central street, the glorious street of the Colonnades, also exactly four miles long, paved for the greater part with blocks of white marble —with its grove of trees, its palaces and shops, and the stately covered colonnade at either side—four miles of shelter from the sun and rain. And, dominating the whole city, the mountain behind, with its highest peak carved into a giant statue of Jupiter, keeping guard over the city, the heathen god claiming this heathen city for his own

Since you cannot get a whole city into your imagination, whenever we come to Antioch in this story, picture this beautiful central street of the Colonnades, with its branching side streets, and the mighty Jupiter dominating it all.

The inhabitants were mainly the peoples that I have pictured to you already—the Greek, the Roman, and the Jew. The Greek, who had lost his faith in his beautiful gods ; the Roman, satiated with his lust of pride of mastery ; the Jew, in his haughty claim to be the sole favourite of the Almighty, standing coldly aloof. The Jewish religion, therefore, had little real influence. The only religion that counted at all was the so-called worship of the ancient gods, the deification of cruelty and lust. Surely, that beautiful, proud city of Antioch sorely needed the gospel of Jesus Christ.

III

How did Christianity first touch Antioch? Through the providence of God. Through the blunders of Saul and his friends. In the persecution that arose about Stephen the hunted disciples travelled as far as Antioch, "speaking the word to none save only the Jews." Notice that phrase: "speaking only to the Jews." Thereby hangs a tale to be told later on. But the river of the water of life could not be held by such boundaries. The Gentiles wanted to hear, and some men of Cyprus and Cyrene, who had not the strict prejudice of the Jerusalem Jews, ventured to preach to the Gentiles.

The results were startling. The people came crowding in: "The hand of the Lord was with them, and a great number believed and turned to the Lord." And immediately there arose a problem and a controversy which afterwards shook the Church to its foundations. Shall Israel lose its peculiar glory and be merged with other races in the church of the Messiah? Shall the uncircumcised heathen be admitted to the Church on a level with the ancient people of God? Must they not first be circumcised and be obedient to the law? Must they not first become members of the Jewish Church? Keep this in mind if you would understand the Epistle of St. Paul.

The news about the Antioch Mission reached the heads of the Church at Jerusalem. They had had to face the question already. Peter, in the teeth of his own prejudices, had felt impelled to baptise the heathen centurion, Cornelius, because he saw the visible sign of God's approval. The gift of the Holy Ghost had come on Cornelius and his house. The Jerusalem Christians immediately challenged his action and brought him before the Apostolic Council. Peter related the whole story and defended himself : " What else could I do ? " he asked. " Who am I that I should withstand God ? " And the Apostles and the brethren listened in wonder. Their prejudices also were strong against such action, but when they had heard they held their peace and glorified God and said, " Then hath God also to the Gentiles granted repentance unto life." It was evidently a new idea to them.

Now came to them the news from Antioch, and they decided to send down a delegate to look into it, and they chose Saul's friend, Joseph Barnabas. You remember Barnabas, the man who introduced Saul to the Apostles when they declined to see him. The story suggests that he was an old friend—perhaps a friend of his college days. Since he is prominent in the later story you need to know him, to recognise him when you see him.

IV

As I see him he is quite a contrast to his friend. Barnabas is built in a large mould—a big, handsome, bearded man, with honest eyes, and what we call a good face—a face to be trusted at first sight. He is a bright, cheery, comforting sort of man—straight, simple, not particularly clever, but very sympathetic, and, above all, a man of deep and real religion. That is Barnabas. Just the right friend for a man like Paul. You get hints for his portrait here and there through the Acts if you use your imagination as you read. You find that the wild highlanders of Lycaonia one day mistook him and Paul for gods. They called Barnabas Jupiter—the stately, majestic father of the gods; and they called Paul Mercury —the small, swift, eloquent message of Olympus. That gives you at once the appearance of the two men.

As to his character. We first hear definitely of him at Jerusalem, when the young Church in its first enthusiasm started what seems to have been an unwise experiment in Socialism—rich and poor to share and share alike. It did not work, but Barnabas took part and sold his estate for the poor and brought the money and laid it at the Apostles' feet (what Ananias and Sapphira pretended to do). Only a generous enthusiast would do that. Next I notice that he must have been a very kindly, sympathetic man, for the Apostles named him Barnabas, the Son of Consolation. And soon after, St. Luke expresses the opinion of the Church, " He was a good man and full of the Holy Ghost."

v

Barnabas came to Antioch and saw the street of the Colonnades and the great statue of the god, but he was more interested in the side street where the Christians met. It was called Singon Street in the old Church traditions. " When he came," I read, " and had seen the grace of God, he was glad, and exhorted them all with purpose of heart they should cleave unto the Lord." He evidently kept clear of the burning question of the day. He did not tell them to be circumcised or to become Jews. He was a simple man, but he saw through to the essentials. " Cleave unto the Lord," he said. That was his religion.

But still the controversy did not cease. The problem was there still, and Barnabas probably felt that he was not a big enough man to handle it, and he knew the man who could handle it. There was no petty jealousy in Barnabas. " Then departed Barnabas to Tarsus to seek Saul." One day in Tarsus, Saul, restless and despondent, suddenly came on his big friend in the street. " Saul, you are needed ; come back with me to Antioch."

The hour had struck. The man was ready. Saul of Tarsus had found his life work.

VI

A year has elapsed. The Christians of Antioch are assembled with their presbyters in Singon Street for a special service of prayer and fasting, and waiting for guidance from the Holy Spirit for a special undertaking which they had in mind—" While they ministered before the Lord fasting." The Greek word used for their ministrations is that from which we derive our word Liturgy—our word for the Communion office. We need not discuss it further here. Naturally, the Holy Communion, the central service, would be the chief part.

What were the special devotions for ?

During the past year Saul and Barnabas had ministered in the city. We are only told that for a whole
year " they assembled with the Church and taught
much people." It was probably a happy, restful time
in Saul's troubled life, going in and out with his old
friend in quiet pastoral duties, and it seems to have
been a successful year too, for we find five prominent
ministers now in Antioch.

We, after nineteen centuries of Christianity, can
never realise all it meant to man when it was new.
It is an old story with us. It was new tidings to
them—tidings of wonder, and joy, and hope. " We
know that the Son of God is come. We believe in
the forgiveness of sins and the resurrection of the dead,
and the life of the world to come. We believe in the
Holy Ghost, the Lord and Giver of Life."

And all that year it would seem that the feeling
had been growing that they must spread the good news.
" This is the day of good tidings and we hold our
peace. The whole heathen world is around us dreary
and helpless and sinful as we were a year ago. We
must go and tell them." They believe that this
strong impulse is from the Holy Ghost. Now they
are waiting for His further guidance. Whom shall
they send ?

Watch the congregation assembled with their five
clergy   Three white men, two black men from Africa.
Read the list in Acts xiii., 1-7. Barnabas and Lucius
of Cyrene, and Simeon that was called Niger or black,
and Manaen the foster-brother of Herod the tetrarch,
and Saul. I like to look at the group. First, the tall
handsome Barnabas ; next to him, a coloured man
Lucius of Cyrene, an African town ; next to him,

Simeon Niger or negro—not what we know as negro—the northern African was a different type. Was he also of Cyrene like Lucius? Simon, the Cyrenian? Was he Simon the Cyrenian, who carried the cross for Jesus on the way to Calvary? I think it quite probable, though I have never seen it suggested before, and the evidence is only the probability that I refer to. If I am right, cannot you imagine his interest in Christianity? Next to him the foster-brother of King Herod. That set us thinking. Just think of it. Two boys mothered at the same breast. One a tyrant, an adulterer, a murderer, the other a preacher of the Gospel of Christ. To these add Saul of Tarsus, and I think you have as interesting a group of clergy as you have ever seen.

Now, then, who is to go on the heathen mission? Black or White? Doubtless they drew lots, as at the election of Matthias. They asked the Holy Ghost to guide them by the lot. That I think is the meaning of the words: "The Holy Ghost said separate me Barnabas and Saul."

Barnabas and Saul! The congregation had prayed for guidance, but I wonder if they liked the answer?

The beloved Barnabas, the brilliant Saul, the very pick of the Antioch ministers! Are they to lose their best? I think that only their deep belief in the presence of the Holy Ghost restrained their murmuring. I have heard a good deal of such murmuring in the Old Country, when the most brilliant of our clergy were sent to the mission field. I have heard over and over (you have heard it too), " are there not plenty of heathen at home? "

There is here a great missionary lesson for the

Church. Were there not plenty of heathen at home,
there in a city of 500,000 ?   But they, at least, were
within reach of the good news, whether they cared for
it or not.   The poor outside heathen had no chance
at all.   And so the Holy Spirit of God spake in their
hearts. " Sacrifice yourselves. Send them your best."
Think of it to-day in the Church's missionary work.
Six hundred millions of these heathens in the world
still.

The Church instantly bowed to the decision.   They
laid their hands on them in loving benediction, and the
two friends went away together on their perilous
journey of three long years.

VII

Next chapter we shall follow them on that journey.
Now let us linger a little in Antioch.   Paul and Barnabas are gone.   Three clergy remain—the two Africans
and the king's foster-brother, but the Church kept
growing—growing fast. The next words indicate
it, " and the disciples were called Christians first in
Antioch." The name we Gentiles glory in to-day was
started that year in Singon Street in the city of the
Street of the Colonnades.   I do not think it originated
with Christians.   They called themselves the Disciples,
the Brethren, the Saints.   It certainly did not originate
with the Jews, who would never give a name
acknowledging the Christ.   They called them " the
sect of the Nazarenes."

It must have come from the general public, who had
to have some name for these people who were beginning
to be talked about.   Probably it began as a nickname

in the slang of the town, but it shows that they were becoming important, and since they embraced every race and every colour, they had to have a comprehensive title.   Black or white, rich or poor, male or female, Greek, or Roman, or Jew, their one distinguishing mark was that they were followers of the Christ.   Let us not forget why we are called Christians.

VIII

They grew so fast that in a few years later they had in Antioch the full organisation of the Church—bishop, priests and deacons, without which there was no church of Christ anywhere in the world for 1,500 years.   Have you ever heard of St. Ignatius of Antioch, the most famous of the early bishops ?   He was born in the lifetime of St. Paul.   He was a disciple of St. John.   He was fifteen years old at the time of that missionary service in Singon Street.   I wonder if the boy was there that day.   About thirty years later he was consecrated Bishop of Antioch, and thirty years later still he was flung to the lions in the Roman amphitheatre. One of the most pathetic stories in history is the story of that dear old Bishop of Antioch going up to die. On the way they had to rest at Smyrna, where Polycarp, a disciple of St. John, was bishop—and the bishops of Ephesus and Magnesia, with several presbyters and deacons, came to receive his blessing, and the old man wrote letters to the Churches around.

Let me give you a few sentences out of these epistles of Ignatius.   He was very uneasy lest the unity of the Church should be broken—lest sects and divisions should arrive when he was gone.   To keep the unity,

he says, cling to your bishops.   They are the guardians
of unity.

" Remember in your prayer the Church of Syria,
which now has God for its Shepherd instead of me.
Jesus Christ must be its Bishop when I am gone."

" Keep in unity with your bishops and presbyters
and deacons, who have been appointed according to the
mind of Jesus Christ.   Apart from that there is no
Church.   Do nothing without your bishops, who, to
the uttermost bounds of the earth, are according to the
will of Jesus Christ.   Reverence your bishop as you
would the Lord Himself.   Reverence your presbyters
as the holy apostles."

It is no part of my purpose now to discuss this
subject.   Some day I hope to lecture fully about it,
but I cannot pass from the Church of Antioch without
referring to it.   It has become a very important subject
in recent years owing to the earnest efforts of Christian
people towards reunion, especially the great Faith and
Order Movement started in America.   Since three-
fourths of all Christendom is under episcopal rule the
question of the episcopate has to be discussed.   And
there is no more hopeful sign of the sincerity of these
movements than the frank, candid way it is being
approached on all sides.

THE MASTER BUILDER

C

PART III

THE MASTER BUILDER

CHAPTER VI

THE FIGHT FOR FREEDOM

PAUL and Barnabas are starting out on the Church's first missionary expedition to the heathen. Watch them as they start, with some of their church people seeing them off, from Singon Street, through the street of the Colonnades, under the colossal shadow of Jupiter, to the pier of Seleucia, which is visible still on clear days down under the sea.

I think they are happy as the ship glides out into the deep blue Mediterranean. For they are two close friends going off together, and they are young enough yet to feel the thrill of an unknown adventure, and they have a mission that rouses their highest enthusiasm, and they know, as few other men have known, the certainty that they are sent by God. And another pleasant thing, to Barnabas at least, they have his young cousin, John Mark, as their attendant. You remember John Mark in the gospel story. His mother Mary kept open house for the Apostles at Jerusalem,

where they came together in the evening to talk and to
rest.   When Peter escaped from the prison he made
straight for that house, and found his friends there
assembled, praying for him.   Young Mark was evidently a favourite of his.   He called him in an Epistle
" Marcus, my son."   Probably that lad and his mother
knew more of the inner thoughts of the Apostles than
any other family in Jerusalem.

II

So they sailed away from the harbour of Antioch.
Many proud expeditions have left that harbour of
Antioch before and since.   Powerful kings and great
generals, and dashing armies of crusaders.   But
history has forgotten them.   When travellers to-day
are shown the old pier under the sea, it is as the
starting point of three poor humble missionaries going
out to tell the heathen the story of Jesus.

Now I see them landing at Barnabas' old home at
Cyprus, where friends are greeting their big pleasant
friend, and for his sake welcoming his two companions.
Now they are across the island in the white city of
Paphos by the sea, telling their wonderful story.   The
pro-consul, Sergius Paulus, has asked them to Government House to tell it to him.   His evil genius, the
sorcerer Elymas, is present, snarling, fighting hard for
his own hand, defying Paul, blaspheming Jesus, striving
to turn the pro-consul from the faith.   Paul is capable
of pretty strong language when a man does that.   " O,
thou full of all evil and villainy, thou son of the devil,
thou enemy of all righteousness, wilt thou not cease to
pervert the right way of the Lord ?   Behold, the hand

of the Lord is upon thee, thou shalt be blind for a season." Like a whipped cur the sorcerer fled, " and the pro-consul believed and turned to the Lord."

Whatever the reason, one is conscious from this point of a curious change in the story. From this point Paul is the chief figure. Barnabas is moving into the background. And at this point, curiously enough, the name is changed. As Abram became Abraham and Simon became Peter at a crisis in the story of each, so we find at this crisis Saul became Paul. His Jewish name is changed for his Gentile name. Nobody ever calls him anything else in all the rest of his story.

III

From Cyprus they follow the course of the trading ships to Perga, on the mainland, and here an unpleasant incident occurred, which had very serious results five years later. Young Mark refused to go on. Perhaps he wanted to go back to his mother—perhaps he was frightened at the dangers in front—perhaps he was vexed that his cousin Barnabas was taking second place. At any rate, he took advantage of a homebound ship, and left them there in the lurch, and Paul resented it sharply. He had no use for a shirker.

They continued their journey without him—up the mountain road, into the dangerous interior—across rushing torrents—through passes which were dreaded by the whole country round as the dens of the bandits. What happened to them in those first months no one has told. Perhaps we should place here the perils of rivers and perils of robbers which Paul mentions in his letters later.

The whole expedition occupied probably three years, very slightly sketched for us. As these lectures have to be kept within narrow bounds, I shall only give you two glimpses of them on the road.

The first is to give you a specimen of Paul's preaching. Perhaps a year after leaving Antioch they came to a mountain town of the same name. (They had the emigrant habit there of repeating the names of their native towns.) On the Sabbath they went to the Synagogue service. They sat on the strangers' seat, wearing the Tallith on their heads to indicate that they were Jews, as distinguished from the Gentile proselytes who usually formed part of the congregation. After the Prayers and the reading of the Lessons, the chief rabbi turned courteously to the two strangers, " Sirs, if you have any words of exhortation to the people, say on." That gave Paul his chance. He arose, and making a gesture with his hands to the congregation, began his sermon : " Men of Israel and ye proselytes of the Gentiles, give audience."

Paul was a true orator. A true orator must have some convictions that he would die for if necessary, and he must have the tact to put these convictions attractively. He began by conciliating the Jews, telling the glorious history of the past ; of Jehovah's care and training of this chosen people of God. But he explained that all this glory of the history of the past was but the preparation for the greater glory of the future. He points out that their prophets have borne witness to a great Messiah to come, not to destroy the Law, but to fulfil it. So far the Jews are

with him. Now comes the startling thing. " I am here
to proclaim that the Messiah has come." See, he says,
how he fits in with the old prophecies ; see how the
great forerunner, John the Baptist, was foreseen by
Malachi. True, our leaders at Jerusalem have rejected
and crucified the Messiah, but that too was foretold by
the prophets, " He was to be despised and rejected of
men." They have fulfilled the prophecies in condemn-
ing him.

Then comes the most startling statement of all.
Our rulers blindly killed the Messiah, " but God has
raised Him from the dead." (You can feel the audience
catching their breath.) That, too, is part of your
prophecies. " Thou shalt not suffer thine Holy One
to see corruption." That resurrection, he says, is
God's greatest proof. After His resurrection He was
seen for many days by those who were with Him, who
are now His witnesses to the people of Israel.

v

No wonder they were stirred. A pretty fair amount
of excitement for one sermon. And he closes with
solemn, daring words : " Be it known unto you, therefore, men and brethren, that through this Jesus is
proclaimed unto you the forgiveness of sins—and in
Him all who have faith are justified from all trans-
gressions. Beware, therefore, lest that come upon
you which is spoken by our prophet Habakkuk,
' Behold ye despisers, and wonder and perish. For I
work a work in your days, a work which ye shall in no
wise believe, though a man declare it unto you.' "

That gives you the general line of Paul's sermons
to Jews. With Gentiles he takes a different line, as
we shall see later. Paul had not failed this time.
He left them gasping with excitement. The congregation crowded around him beseeching him to stay
and repeat these things next Sabbath. All the week
they talked of nothing else, and on the next Sabbath
"came almost the whole city together to hear the
word of God." The synagogue was crowded to the
doors and beyond, but many of that crowd were
Gentiles. Paul had hinted that his message was for
all—that the Messiah was for all. The Jews could not
stand that. They, too, had been talking together all the
week. They came into church angry and embittered.
The prayers were spoiled for them, everything was
spoiled. When Paul arose to speak he was greeted
with howls and curses. As he argued they sprang
up in fierce opposition, contradicting and blaspheming.

Paul bore it as long as he could. Then, with a stern
gesture, he forced them into silence. He had to decide
quickly. In a moment during the uproar he made
the decision of his life—a decision which caused a
perfect revolution in the church of the future. In
slow measured words, tense with restrained emotion,
he announces it, " It was necessary that the word of
God should first have been spoken to you ; but seeing
that ye put it from you, and judge yourselves unworthy
of everlasting life, lo, we turn to the Gentiles. For so
hath the Word commanded us, saying, ' I have sent
thee to be the light of the Gentiles, that thou shouldest
be for salvation unto the ends of the earth.' "

That sermon marked a crisis for Paul and for the

Church. That day Paul nailed his colours to the mast. " The Jew is no longer the sole favourite of God. The Church is for all the world." To us that is a mere truism. To the Jewish world of Paul's day it was nothing less than a revolution.

After that there was no staying in Pisidia. The Jews stirred up the honourable women, and in all ages when the honourable women get after a man he may as well get out. The honourable women stirred up the honourable men, and the missionaries were driven across the border.

VI

Away in the mountains three months later we have another glimpse of the expedition. It is the mountain town of Lystra. It seems a festival or market day, for the town is crowded. Paul is preaching in a public place. In his audience is a poor cripple whose wistful eyes are holding the preacher. He positively cannot get on with his sermon with these pathetic eyes on him. Paul, looking earnestly on him, and perceiving that he had the faith to be healed, cried with a loud voice, " Stand upright on thy feet," and he leaped and walked, and the people cried out in the speech of Lycaonia, " The gods are come down to us in the likeness of men." And they called Barnabas Jupiter (from his stately appearance), and Paul Mercurius, because he was the chief speaker. And the priest of Jupiter brought oxen and garlands, and would have done sacrifice with the people, but Barnabas and Paul rent their garments and rushed in among the crowd, ' Sirs, why do ye these things ? We also are men of like passions with you, and preach unto you that ye should turn from these vanities unto the living God, which made heaven and earth, and the sea, and all the things that are therein."

Not quite so tactful as his sermon in Pisidia.

It is dangerous to meddle with the passions of a mob. It is dangerous to call their gods vain things ; it is dangerous in the midst of their superstitious emotions, when they want to worship you, to make them feel ridiculous by having mistaken you for a god. Mobs are ticklish things to handle. This crowd grows silent, grows sulky ; begins to listen to the hostile Jews from Iconium. " If they are not gods, then they healed the cripple by the power of the Evil One." So when Paul tried to preach next day he could scent trouble in the air. He found a changed atmosphere. The crowd is hostile. Soon the yelling roughs from the back lanes are jostling and crowding around him. Soon the stones are flying. He sees that there is no escape. He is hit. He is down. His eyes are closed, but his brain is forming vivid pictures of another stoning twelve years before in which he himself took part, and a dead face, that was as the face of an angel. Soon a stunning blow on the head sends his pictures flying, and Barnabas is looking on another dead face, and looking out into the lonely years without his comrade. But Paul is not dead. It would take more than that to kill him while his great life work remained undone.

And here is a very interesting coincidence. Twelve years ago the young Paul had been a spectator at the stoning of Stephen, and largely as the result of that stoning the Church had gained her doughtiest champion. This day a frightened lad is spectator at the stoning of Paul—a Lystra boy living with his mother and grandmother, and largely as a result of that stoning, Paul is going to win his best fellow-worker, to be to him as a son in his old age. We hear nothing of him here, but two years afterwards, in passing through this town of Lystra, Paul finds young Timothy a convert of his own. Long years afterwards, when Timothy is a bishop, Paul writes to him praising the religious influence of his mother, Eunice, and his grandmother, Lois, and he reminds him, " Remember, Timothy, what I suffered in Lystra." So you see there is little doubt that he was there at the stoning.

We cannot follow this journey in further detail. When they reached Derbe they stopped and turned back in their tracks—over all the towns where they preached the gospel. They made choice of fit persons to serve in the sacred ministry of the Church and ordained presbyters in every city. These presbyters could not do much preaching. They did not know much themselves, but they could remember and repeat what was carefully taught to them, and they could administer the sacraments as the Lord commanded. Thus ends the first missionary journey.

VIII

So they return to Antioch, under the shadow of Jupiter, across the Street of the Colonnades, down to Singon Street, and there at the gathering of the church which had sent them out three years ago, we are told in two lines, " they rehearsed all that God had done with them and how He had opened a door of faith unto the Gentiles." You can easily imagine for yourselves the interest of that meeting. I have no time for it now.

I am thinking, rather, of the night time, when the meeting was over and Paul and Barnabas were talking privately with the chief lay people and with the clergy, the two Africans and the king's foster-brother : " How are things doing here in Antioch ? " " Very badly ; they could hardly be worse. There is trouble ahead." " What is the trouble ? " " O, just the old trouble with the Jerusalem people, but now things are coming to a crisis. A little while ago certain men came down from Jerusalem and taught the brethren here, ' Except ye be circumcised after the custom of Moses ye cannot be saved.' Our Gentile converts are puzzled and irritated. We have been teaching them free salvation for Jew and Gentile who cleave unto the Lord. Those men say we are wrong ; that these brethren must be circumcised and obey the Jewish ordinances. So things are pretty miserable. If something is not done soon we are likely to have the Church split in two."

Evidently it was quite time Paul and Barnabas got back. The big fight was on everywhere. Not only away in their lonely mission, but here in Antioch, and in Jerusalem—all over the Church. It was a fight for liberty, and Paul set his face grimly to fight it to a finish. He would not let his Gentile converts be dragged under the yoke of Judaism. He would not let Christianity become a Jewish sect. He flung out his challenge, which later he repeated: " Stand fast, therefore, in the liberty wherewith Christ hath made you free, and be not entangled with the yoke of bondage."

IX

To understand Paul's lifelong fight for liberty in the Church you must try to understand his opponents. They, too, had their deep religious convictions. The divine law of the Jews demanded isolation from the heathen. The idolatry and abominable immorality of heathendom made it necessary. " Come ye out from among them and touch not the unclean thing." Touch not, taste not, handle not. It was just like the law of caste in India. As Peter said to Cornelius, " It is unlawful for a man who is a Jew to keep company or come unto one of another nation." The only way in which a Gentile could join in the worship of Jehovah was by becoming a proselyte and obeying the Jewish ordinances. Mark you, this was the law of God—the rule of religion for a thousand years. Naturally they felt that this must go on. The Jewish Christians thought that Christianity should be just a purer, holier form of Judaism.

Now comes this revolutionary Paul. He says no, the old law was only for a limited time—only a preparation for the kingdom of the Messiah. Christ is the Messiah, not for Israel only, but for the whole of humanity. When the Gentile comes to Christ, when his idolatry is abandoned and his immorality gone, Jew and Gentile stand equal as brothers in the universal Church.

There is the whole question. Both sides claim the authority of God. Both were equally determined. In the face of this difficulty how was there ever to be a united Church ? The solution of the problem seemed in that day almost impossible, and without the intervention of God's grace on His servants it would have been impossible. But God gave to the Apostles the wisdom and discretion and firmness necessary, and through His grace Paul became the great instrument in accomplishing a work necessary to the very existence of a Catholic—a Universal Church.

You see, Paul was determined to fight, and Paul felt he could win, but he saw it would not do to win at the cost of splitting the Church in two—a Jewish Christian Church, with its centre at Jerusalem ; and a Gentile Christian Church, with its centre at Antioch. The Church in all ages needs not merely determined fighters for right, but also reasonable, sympathetic, statesman-like men, who will go and talk things over with the other man, and try to understand his position.

Clearly there must be no schism, and clearly the whole position must be taken before the heads of the Church. So I read, " the brethren appointed Paul and Barnabas and certain others to go up to Jerusalem to the Apostles and elders about this question."

X

Now we are in Jerusalem. It is the first synod of the Catholic Church. Not in a stately synod hall. Probably in the upper room of the house of John Mark's mother. But no stately council of Nice or Trent had so vital an issue before it. No doubt it had been prefaced by very earnest prayer. As far as we can judge, James, who was Bishop of Jerusalem, presided, and since he was known to be a very strict Jew, I dare say Paul's opponents hoped much from his position. Both sides evidently tried to win adherents. There is a great deal of human nature even in Church synods. Now the lists are set, the big fight is on.

I read, " After there had been much questioning." I know enough about Synods with burning questions to know what that meant. The attack of the Judaisers, the replies of their opponents, strong arguments and sometimes hot words—a long, eager controversy—probably for hours. Then the Apostles rose to speak, and the multitude kept silence.

Peter was the first speaker. He spoke strongly against the Judaisers and in favour of Paul : " You are well aware," he said, " that these heathen in Syria are not the first heathen who have come to the Church. I myself was chosen by God to begin this work, which Paul is continuing. You know how I baptised the heathen centurion Cornelius, how God, which knoweth the heart, bear them witness, giving them the Holy Ghost even as He did unto us. He made no distinction between us and them. Now, therefore, why tempt ye God, putting a yoke on the necks of the disciples, which neither our fathers nor we are able to bear We believe that they and we together shall be saved in the same way through the grace of the Lord Jesus."

That was a hard knock for the Judaisers. However, there was still hope, James had not spoken yet. Then Paul and Barnabas were called, and all the multitude kept silence and hearkened unto Barnabas and Paul, rehearsing what wonders God had wrought among the Gentiles by them. You can imagine how eloquently Paul fought his cause.

And after they had held their peace, James arose. This was the sensational moment. Both sides waited with bated breath for his decision. No judgment would have such weight with the Judaising party as his. He was a thorough Jew—if anything, a narrow Jew. In garb and appearance he was like John the Baptist, a stern, silent, deeply holy man, with the bare feet and unshorn head of the Nazarite.

When James arose and solemnly pronounced that the Mosaic customs were not of eternal obligation, and that he agreed with Peter and with Paul, that practically closed the question. The Council closed in a spirit of charity and mutual forbearance. They had sought the guidance of the Holy Spirit ; they accepted this as His guidance, and Paul and Barnabas were sent back happy to their church in Antioch, carrying this Apostolic letter as their authority if there should be further trouble :

" The Apostles and elders unto the brethren of the Gentiles in Antioch, and Syria, and Cilicia, greeting : For much as we have heard that certain which went out from us have troubled you with words subverting your souls, it seemed good unto us to send Silas and others with our beloved Barnabas and Paul, who have hazarded their lives for the name of Our Lord Jesus Christ.

"It seemed good to the Holy Ghost and to us to lay upon you no greater burden than these necessary things : that ye abstain from meats offered to idols, and from blood, and from things strangled, and from the fornication, from which if ye keep yourselves ye shall do well. Fare ye well."

CHAPTER VII

SECOND MISSIONARY TOUR

HAPPY and triumphant after their signal victory at the Council of Jerusalem, Paul and Barnabas returned to Antioch, and there I read, " they tarried teaching and preaching the word of the Lord with many others also." Amongst these others were Silas, who had been sent with them from Jerusalem by the Apostles, and also, as we learn from the Epistle to the Galatians, Peter, who on one of his tours had come down to Antioch, and brought with him his young favourite, John Mark. You remember young Mark, who had deserted Paul and Barnabas on their first missionary expedition.

" Paul and Barnabas tarried together in Antioch." In the light of later history that little statement is pathetic. The two old friends, after their three years missionary tour, after winning side by side the fight for the Church's freedom, were now living happily together in the quiet comradeship of pastoral work in Antioch. How little they thought that it would be their last year together. That before the year was over there should come through their own fault a break in that close friendship which should part them, never again to meet on earth

It is a sorrowful story, but very human. Two most unpleasant incidents spoiled what should have been one of the happiest years of their life.

II

Paul and Barnabas, and Silas, and Peter, and Mark, and the king's foster-brother, and the two Africans, were working happily together, rejoicing in their new freedom, living in pleasant intercourse with Jew and Gentile converts alike, when one day another band of the bigoted Christian Jews came down from Jerusalem. They dared not oppose the Apostolic decree, but by their haughty, stand-off attitude toward the Gentile converts they made things very unpleasant.

Paul could stand this all right so long as his comrades stood by him, but soon to his surprise he sees Peter wavering. Peter had fought bravely beside him for the equality of the Jew and the Gentile in the Church, but it is not easy for men to shake off altogether the prejudices of a lifetime. Peter in this city of strangers naturally associated much with the Jerusalem people who were old acquaintances, and soon there were signs that he was leaning to their side. The other Christian Jews were influenced by Peter, even Barnabas began to keep aloof from the Gentile converts. Naturally these converts were very much hurt. Paul bore with it as long as he could, but he soon saw that a determined stand must be taken, even at the risk of vexing his comrades.

There is no word of all this in the history, but ten years afterwards Paul tells it in his Galatian letter: " But when Peter was come to Antioch, I withstood him to the face, because he was to be blamed. For before that certain men came from James he did eat with the Gentiles, but when they were come he withdrew and separated, fearing them which were of the circumcision. And the other Jews dissembled likewise with him ; insomuch that Barnabas also was carried away with their dissimulation. But when I saw that they walked not uprightly according to the truth of the Gospel, I said unto Peter before them all, if thou, being a Jew, etc." *

It was a hard thing for Paul to rebuke his closest friends in a public assembly, but hard things have to be done. Evidently his action was effective. Barnabas and Peter were doubtless big enough men to acknowledge their fault, and so the situation was saved, but I cannot help suspecting that it made a little rift within the lute, which accounts for later troubles. Public rebukes are not easily forgotten even by good men.

III

Three months later the next trouble came. It is time for Paul and Barnabas to set out again on the next missionary journey. Barnabas very much wants to take his young cousin, John Mark, again. " No," said Paul, " I cannot trust any man who deserted us as he did. This work of God is too serious to be injured by shirkers. I will not have young Mark again." Barnabas pleaded, Paul was determined—neither would give in. Probably the recent wavering of Peter and Barnabas was referred to. One word brought on

* Gal. ii. : 14.

another, " and the contention was so sharp between them that they separated one from the other," never to meet again. It is a sorrowful story, but, alas, it is so human that we can easily understand it. The very depth of their affection made the contention the sharper. Each thought the other should yield. So

> " Each spake words of high disdain,
> Sharp words that hurt his heart's best brother
> But never either found another,
> To keep the lonely heart from pain.
> Like cliffs that had been rent asunder,
> They parted not to meet again."

The Bible is very candid about the failure of its heroes, and it is some comfort to us, who are very faulty, that God can make saints out of very faulty people. But it would be happy for us if our quarrels had as noble a cause. It was no selfish quarrel as to who should be more successful, or who should gain something. It was just a difference as to the best way of serving Christ, whether by the gentler way of indulgence to young Mark, or by the sterner way of putting Mark aside. Well for us if our quarrels had no worse ground than that.

You may be sure Paul often looked back to the days when that faithful comrade stood by him when others suspected him, especially to that never-to-be-forgotten day when he found his life work, when " Barnabas came to Tarsus to seek Saul." You may be sure Barnabas, too, thought regretfully of those days of loving comradeship.

It is pleasant to look forward to later years when Paul writes affectionately of his old comrade—when Peter writes of the Epistles " of our beloved brother

Paul "—when Paul found that young Mark was a better man than he had thought : " Bring Mark to me ; he is profitable to the ministry."* And it is some comfort for faulty people like ourselves to see that God could make holy saints out of these faulty men.

IV

At any rate God's work must not suffer. So Barnabas took Mark and sailed into Cyprus, where an old tradition says that he died for his Lord ; and Paul chose Silas. I am sure Silas was a wise friend and a valuable missionary. But he was not Barnabas.

I think Paul was already feeling the stir of that ambitious impulse which afterwards took him ever westward, westward ; took him to Rome, even to Spain, to the bounds of the Empire, to plant there the banner of his beloved Lord. Soon he saw clear signs that God was so guiding him. They started by land up through the northern highlands, out through the dark defiles of the Cilician gates, that great frowning pass, eighty miles long. Then westward for days along the mountain road, till he touched the region of his first missionary journey. One evening from the heights he looked down on Derbe and rejoiced that he was to meet the old friends again. Next day along the mountain road to Lystra, where Barnabas and he had been Jupiter and Mercury, and where Barnabas had lifted him up for dead after the mob had stoned him. Everything would remind him of Barnabas.

I can easily picture these visits. Recently with

* 2 Tim. iv. : 11.

the Bishop of Montreal I called on Archbishop
Germanos of the Syrian Church, who was visiting his
churches in Canada and the United States.   In a
street off Notre Dame I found him staying with one
of his Syrian people.   He was sitting in his black robes
with his presbyters beside him, and his people were
crowding in to greet him and to consult him.   It was
a picture from the unchanging East.

It was just Paul over again.   I see him come in to
Lystra and the converts crowd around him delighted
to see him, and I am sure the first question is, Where
is Barnabas ?   And the next is, Have you recovered
from the effects of the stoning ?   And so they talk
together in affectionate intercourse, and Silas is introduced, and at night the presbyters bring their difficulties to be solved, and are taught still further of the
Gospel of Christ ; for they do not know very much,
these presbyters, and there are no written Gospel.
as yet to teach them.

Among the visitors that day was probably young
Timothy, who lived with his mother and grandmother
on the Iconium road.   Paul seems to have known him
at his previous visit.   He had probably been present
when Paul was stoned.   He must have been a very
attractive lad, for the older man was greatly drawn to
him.

From all the disciples at Lystra he singled him out ;
" Him Paul would have go forth with him."   He was
a lonely man, with a tender, affectionate heart, and it
would be delightful to have with him and to have the
training of this youth who seemed to love him already,
and who might be to him in his old age his son in
the Gospel.

So he inquires of the presbyters and friends, " What do you think of Timothy ? Is he a man to make a presbyter ? Is he a man to take with me ? " And they reply, " He is well reported of by the brethren at Iconium." So he directs him to be circumcised, since his mother is a Jewess. He arranges for his ordination, since he will have to admininster the sacraments. Perhaps at Lystra or at Iconium the following Sunday that solemn ordination took place. Many years afterwards, towards the close of his life, he writes to Timothy, who had become to him all or more than he had ever hoped, and who at that time was himself a Bishop of the Church : " I thank God for thee my son Timothy, unceasing is my remembrance of thee in my prayers. Night and day I am longing to see thee. I remember the faith of the grandmother Lois and thy mother Eunice. Stir up the gift of God that is in thee through the laying on of my hands, together with the hands of the presbytery."* " You know what I suffered in Lystra."

V

But Paul cannot delay with his friends at Lystra. A higher power is compelling him westward—ever westward. St. Luke has so set his eyes on the western goal that he will not take time to tell what happened on the way. " They went through Galatia," he says. Evidently Paul meant to go through without stopping. The historian does not tell that there came on him a sudden, sharp attack, probably of that old malady— that loathsome " thorn in the flesh " which he refers

* 1 Tim. i. : 14 ; 2 Tim. i. : 6.

to in his letters, which so prostrated and humiliated him whenever it occurred. It is generally believed to be a disfiguring affection of the eyes, accompanied with horrible pain, like a stake driven through the flesh.

We only know of this stay of Paul amongst the Galatians through a letter which he wrote them afterward. It is a stern letter of rebuke for their fickleness, and in it he affectionately recalls his first visit, and their loving reception of the poor, sick stranger in a strange land : " Ye did not despise me or loath me in my humiliating malady. Ye listened to my teaching on my sick bed, as if I were an angel of God. I bear you witness that ye would have plucked out your own eyes and given them to me if it would do me any good. Why have ye changed ? O, foolish Galatians, who hath bewitched you, that ye have so soon turned aside ?" It is a most interesting sidelight, showing the intense earnestness of a man in the misery of his sickness telling these wild Galatian tribes the glorious news about Jesus.

By the way, these Galatians ought to be the most interesting to us of all Paul's converts. They are the nearest race to ourselves of all whom Paul had met. The others are Greeks and Romans, and Jews and Eastern tribes. These are the people whose kinsmen we know. Galatians is the Greek name for Gauls. The Greeks called the inhabitants of Western France, Galatians. The Romans called them Gauls. Their old name is Celts. They are the Celtic people who inhabited France and Ireland. The Epistle to the Galatians is the Epistle to the Gauls—to the kindred of the wild Irish in the ancient world. And Paul found in them the same characteristics, the same loving, affectionate hearts for the sick stranger in trouble, the same impetuous nature, the same fickleness which he rebukes, the fighting and devouring which he bids them avoid.   Fighting is in the very nature of the Celt.   To Irish and other Celts to-day it should be interesting to find their ancient kinsmen nursing St. Paul.   I hope it will make them read the Epistle to the Galatians.

VI

Now the missionaries have left Galatia.   They are moving on westward—westward.   Their route on the map is almost a straight line toward the sunset.   Something is impelling them.   Something happens to stop them at every turn from the path. " We assayed to go into Mysia, but the spirit of Jesus suffered us not.   We were forbidden of the Holy Ghost to preach the word in Asia."   On, on, ever on, toward the West.

At last from the hilltops they catch sight of the sea, and across it the dim outlines of the mountains of Europe.   But Paul and Silas and Timothy are looking on what was much more exciting to the world of their day.   They are looking down upon the Plain of Troas.   Surely Paul as a Roman citizen was stirred at the sight.   Surely young Timothy knew of its romantic associations.   For—do you know where we are ?   We are on the Plains of Troy, the land sung by Homer and Virgil, the cradle of the Roman race, the dreamland of chivalry and romance to the ancient world.   To this day schoolboys everywhere study the classic tale of Priam and Agamemnon, and Helen of Troy, and Achilles dragging dead Hector around the walls.

There is no reference here to these classic glories. I do not think Paul was excited about them as we should be. Put yourself in his place. If you were a courier in the War days hurrying back with the news that Germany had surrendered, and that the liberty of Europe was saved, you would hardly spend a day sentimentalising on the field of Waterloo. Paul was God's courier, with exciting tidings all fresh and new that the Son of God had come; that there was for-giveness of sins; that death was only birth into a fuller life; that humanity was having a splendid new start.

It was all new and fresh and exciting. The poor old world was in sore need of it. Paul could not spend much thought on the glories of Troy.

VII

Here in Troy came another of the close friendships of Paul's life. There was a young physician, probably practising in Troas. Perhaps he came to attend Paul, not yet recovered from his Galatian illness. He was a man of literary taste; he had probably known Paul before. At any rate, he was to know him well in the future. He became to him his friend and companion, his physician in illness, the biographer to whom we owe the story of his life: " Luke, the beloved physician," he calls him, and in the loneliness and depression of the days before his death, when all others had forsaken him, he writes, " only Luke is with me."

Think what it meant to the world this acquaintance with Paul. St. Luke's name has become a household word through all the world, through all the ages. But not as a physician.

Through his acquaintance with Paul, God called him to a greater, wider work—to give to the world the Acts of the Apostles, and the precious Gospel of St. Luke.

How do we know that Luke met Paul at Troas? Because in his history he changes for the first time from the third to the first person. If you are reading the Acts carefully you will find in certain sections " we " instead of " they." Where this occurs we may assume that St. Luke was present.

VIII

We are now in the theatre of the late Great War. The men who have fought around Gallipoli, the allied troops encamped at Salonika, to which afterwards came the Epistles to the Thessalonians, should be interested in this part of the story of St. Paul. They are standing where Paul stood 1900 years earlier. They, too, are standing there for the helping of the world, for the honour of Christ.

Now comes a point in the story of vital interest to ourselves. One evening Paul stood at sunset on the confines of Asia at Troy looking out at the dim mountains of Europe across the sea, and when darkness came—in the visions of the night he learned the meaning of the impulse that was urging him west-ward. The meaning was EUROPE. In Europe was to be planted the banner of the Cross. A vision appeared to Paul in the night—a man of Macedonia beseeching him and saying, " Come over and help us. And straightway we concluded that God had called us to preach the good news unto them. Straightway we sought to go forth." In the morning round the shipping in the harbour were the newly arrived travel-lers seeking a passage. " Setting sail from Troas we made a straight course to Samothrace, and next day to Neapolis, and from thence to Philippi."

Thus came the Gospel to Europe.

of Jesus come, especially in that old world so cruel to women where Jesus would be the more needed?

Chief amongst them was Lydia, a seller of purple robes from Thyatira, whose heart the Lord opened as she gave attention to the things spoken by Paul. Don't you think she deserved it—because she gave attention—because she was there at all.

This was not Jerusalem where the Sabbath was observed. There was no Sabbath in Philippi. It was a heathen city. The shops and bazaars were in full swing. The rival sellers of purple were making their gains. Lydia thought it worth while to lose something in order to worship God, and so she won the blessing of being the first Christian in Europe, and probably had something to do with the founding of the Church in her native town, which you read of in the Epistles to the Seven Churches. " To the angel of the Church in Thyatira write."

So when the Gospel of Jesus came to Europe, it came first to women because the men were not there.

This is a story for women. One likes to get a glimpse of women in their relation to Jesus. Women were the last at His cross when He died. Women were the first at His sepulchre when He rose, and in all the stories of bigotry and hatred and desertion in the gospels there is none of women hostile to Jesus nor of any woman deserting Him. Here women are the first members of His Church in Europe, and in all the ages since they have been the centre and heart of it. The men of Europe have talked and preached and stood more in the limelight, but it is the woman in the home, teaching her little child, that has made the Christianity of Europe.

III

Some months later there is another woman in the story. A poor half-crazy slave girl, a spiritualist medium in touch with unseen mysteries. The Greek poets of that time describe such women. She is in touch with the spirit world. The spirits which touch her are evil, but they give her second sight. She can tell fortunes, and " she brought her masters much gain by soothsaying." Her uncanny knowledge has taught her too much. Day by day wherever they go she follows Paul and Silas with her crazy cry, " These men are the servants of the Most High God, these men are the servants of the Most High God," till at last Paul grieved for the poor girl, and annoyed by her importunity, cast out the evil spirit in the name of Christ. " And her masters saw that the hope of their gains were gone."

Thus came the first assault from the heathen. Paul's enemies up to this had always been Jews. The Jews attacked him when he touched their religion ; the heathen when he touched their pockets.

Next morning Paul is up with Silas before the court, listening to the prosecutor's charge. " These men are Jews ; they are disturbing the city ; they are upsetting religion ; they are teaching things not lawful for us, being Romans." The magistrates make short work of the case, " Strike them, flog them, put them in the dungeon." " How we were shamefully entreated at Philippi," he writes in later years. That is Europe's way of thanking Paul for his gospel.

It was a pretty cruel world in which he lived his outer life, but it was a glorious world in which his

D

spirit lived in the practice of the presence of God
" He endured as seeing Him who is invisible."

> There are in the loud stunning tide
>> Of this world's care and crime,
> With whom the melodies abide
>> Of the everlasting chime.
> Who carry music in their heart
>> Through dusky lane and wrangling mart,
> Who ply their daily task with busier feet
>> Because their secret souls a holier strain repeat.

IV

Such was Paul. That is what made him a hero.
We are proud to-day of the dashing heroism that rushes
fearlessly to the cannon's mouth, but there is higher
heroism in many lives which never get a V.C. or a
D.S.O. Look at this poor little sick Jew who " cut
out the hero stuff " and took it all in the day's work.
Weak, sensitive, highly strung, he is tied to the whip-
ping post and the white flesh flogged to ribbons on his
back. He is flung into the stench of the inner dungeon.
He never whines about such things. He has too
much to be glad about. Look at his whole life—
disappointed, persecuted, deserted, misunderstood—
and then hear the continual refrain of his letters—
" Rejoice in the Lord "—" Rejoicing in tribulation "
—" Our light affliction is but for the moment." " I
have learned," he writes to these people of Philippi,
" in whatsoever state I am therein to be content."

That religion of Christ is worth something if it
makes heroes like that. And it is no unreasoning
fanaticism that makes him brave and cheery. It is

simply commonsense. " What matter if men oppress me ? God is beside me. What matter if my preaching fails this time ? God will win out some day. What matter if they put me to death ? It is but to depart and to be with Christ, which is far better."

The world cannot conquer that sort of man. It cannot even make him very greatly unhappy. " This is the victory that overcometh the world even our faith."

At midnight they were singing hymns unto the Lord, the beautiful old Psalms learned in their childhood, " Praise the Lord, O my Soul." " The Lord hears the mourning of those in captivity."

" And the prisoners were listening." Yes, and the jailer too. It was a new experience to hear the prisoners, instead of howling, singing songs of praise.

I could not do it. Perhaps you could not do it. But you can imagine men of Paul's type, who could see what life really means to every poor servant of Christ, a life only begun on earth, a life of splendid values, of ages of progress, a life that leaves you young when you are older than Methuselah, a life of eternal joyous service in the presence of the Lord. You can imagine such a man looking at his troubles as we look on the little child crying over her broken doll. One day we too shall see it that way.

V

Towards morning came the earthquake shock and the shaking of the prison, and the jailer rushing in to commit suicide believing that his prisoners had fled. He finds Paul and Silas calmly waiting, and one can understand the man's feelings. He knew something already of these men who were proclaiming some wonderful good news, some extraordinary way of salvation. He has seen them flogged yesterday for their teaching. He has heard them singing their doxologies in the night. And there comes on him the awe of the supernatural—the admiration of a brave man for their courage and calmness, the wonder at the curious secret power in their lives. He would like to know the inner meaning of it all. He has little belief in his gods. He has little to comfort him in the troubles of his life. From the depths of his poor soul the question is forced: " Sirs, what must I do to be saved ? Is there any way in which I could be a man such as you ? "

" Believe on the Lord Jesus Christ and thou shalt be saved. And the man believed and his whole house."

Of course, it does not mean that Paul said no more —that an ignorant pagan became Christian in a moment. Paul was not the sort of man to baptise ignorant people. He settled down to teach the man and his family the love of God, the story of Christ, the call of a holy life—the strength of the Holy Ghost through prayer and sacraments. It was an interesting sight as the light fell on the prison walls, and the staring criminals and the blood drying on the apostle's back, as he postponed all thought of comfort and relief in his eagerness to win a poor heathen soul. Surely it made a close tie between them for ever. I like to think of the pleasure to Paul in meeting that friend whenever he revisited Philippi. When I read the Epistle to the Philippians, I like to think of the jailer in church listening to that letter of his friend, the first Sunday after it arrived.

VI

Let us not pass over the jailer's question and its answer. It is hard to guess how much that poor ignorant pagan meant. At any rate he saw the vast difference between his own poor, struggling, dreary life and that of those bright cheery souls who seemed in such friendly intercourse with their gods that they were always happy, who for some secret joy that was set before them made light of flogging and imprisonment and danger and death. " If I could get to be like them ! If I could learn their secret ! What must I do ? "

Perhaps he expected Paul to say you must be good. You must conquer this sin and that, you must acquire this virtue and that. Paul meant him to do all this— but he did not put it that way. " Believe on the Lord Jesus Christ and thou shalt be saved. Join the ranks of my dear Lord, the Lord of Heaven and earth. Put yourself in His hands as I have done and He will do all for you. Offer yourself to Him—let me baptise you into His name—and all the comfort and peace and joy and strength that you see in us will come to you too, and you shall be as we are."

And that poor jailer risked it in simple faith—and Jesus confirmed the promise of His servant—and the new beautiful life began. No wonder with results such as that around him that Paul felt it worth while to suffer for his gospel.

And the Church has gone on ever since with just that same simple gospel. And all through the ages men have been testing its truth. In days of dissatisfaction and aspiration after better things they have asked, What must I do to be saved from my sins, to become pure and noble and generous and true, to be happy in this life and hopeful for the next. And the Church replied, Believe on the Lord Jesus Christ —give yourself to Lord Jesus. And they have tried it as the jailer of Philippi tried it. And the answer has come.

VII

Next day Paul and Silas were banished from Philippi, and had to leave their new friends and new-made converts. It was a great comfort that they were able to leave Luke with them. We are not definitely told that they did. But at this point the narrative, which has been using the first person " we," again changes to " they "—tells only of Paul and Silas going. So we infer that Luke remained behind to watch over that infant community, and perhaps, too, in his spare time, elaborate his notes for his Gospel or for the Acts.

If there were many converts like Lydia and the jailer, religion must have been very real in that little church of Philippi. And apparently it was so. Ten years afterwards Paul writes from a Roman prison his Epistle to the Philippians, the most delightful reading of all his epistles, and from it we learn much. For some reason these Philippians seem nearest to his heart ; they are the only people to whom he writes no reproofs and the only people whom he allowed to minister to him in his necessities. With all others he kept his proud position of earning his own living and refusing all gifts of money.

Evidently in all his troubles Paul had the comfort of very close personal friendships amongst his converts, and especially it would seem in Philippi. Most clergy know that one of the pleasantest things in their ministry is the kindly friendship of their people, even when they very little deserve it.

But what is especially noticeable in the epistle is the close personal relation to Our Lord, both of Paul and his converts, and as a consequence the joyous tone of the whole letter. One sees that the Christian life to them was such a tender, personal relation to the Lord Jesus. He was no dead teacher of noble doctrines. He was the ever present close personal friend, the living, loving Lord for whom they were glad to suffer and would be glad to die. Christianity was a very real thing in the teaching of Paul.

CHAPTER IX

So Paul and Silas came to Salonika. How near Salonika seemed to us in the War days, when the lads dear to ourselves were holding that difficult position, and we studied the pictures of the beautiful old town nestling deep in the mountains by the sea. These young British gunners would have been interested in this chapter if I could have shewn them the path right between their guns where Paul and Silas, sore from the flogging at Philippi, came down that summer morning long ago into the town. It was then called Thessalonica, and to its people afterwards came the very first words of the New Testament ever written, Paul's Epistles to the Thessalonians.

Do you imagine he began by brilliant spectacular preaching? Nay. The first thing was to look for lodgings, and the next to look for work in some tent-maker's shop to cover the expenses of support and travelling. It is only as I look closely into his life that I realise what a hero Paul was. In the keen strain of clerical life I wonder how long I should stand it if I had to sit up at night to cut and stitch tentcloth to earn my breakfast—if I had a chronic disease—if I

was persecuted and disliked—and if I varied the
monotony by getting stoned or flogged once a year. I
might do it for the sake of someone whom I greatly
loved. It helps me to see how much a man can do
who is intensely in earnest. It helps me to estimate
how deep was this man's love to the Lord who had been
so good to him on the Damascus road. Those months
of study are helping me to appreciate and admire Paul
as I never did before.

II

As his custom was everywhere, he began his teaching in the Jewish Synagogue, where he and his audience
had their Bible, the Old Testament, as common ground.
Here he argues from the Scriptures that their idea of
a Messiah, glorious in temporal power, was an error—
" opening and alleging that it behoved the Christ to
suffer and to rise again from the dead, and that this
Jesus whom I proclaim unto you is the promised
Messiah." It was the very line that Jesus took with
the disciples at Emmaus on Easter day, " Ought not
the Christ to have suffered these things and entered
into His glory. And thus He interpreted to them in
all the Scriptures the things concerning Himself."

It was a hard proposition for Jews. For ages the
national hope had been fed on glowing pictures of the
Messiah and His brilliant reign, ignoring all the hints
of suffering and humiliation, how He should bear our
griefs and carry our sorrows. Indeed, it is only through
the life of Christ and the teaching of the Apostles
that that side of the picture has come out into
prominence.

" And some were persuaded "—and some were not. It is so in all preaching, and depends largely on the attitude of the hearers towards the right. Even Paul could not make some men care. I notice that the believers were chiefly Greek proselytes, who were admitted to the synagogues as a sort of inferior outer circle. And you can see why. The Jews had a great religion already. The poor Greeks had nothing but the fables about gods, in whom they had lost belief, and who could never be any help to an earnest soul. If Paul's gospel were true—if God were really in close touch with men, as Paul said He was, it was delightful news for them in their sore need of Him.

Then came the old trouble. The unbelieving Jews stirred up the rabble, the loafers and idlers, the lewd fellows of the baser sort. The mob was in a riot. Paul could not show his face in the streets. After about two months he had to go.

One would expect the little church to die out now when its great leaders are gone. Far from it. Here we see the innate power of the Gospel as Christ predicted. " Like seed," He says, " sown in the ground." Like seed. For the seed has in it a hidden life, you cannot hold it back. It must grow. Throw a handful of seeds on the ground and neglect them. They will grow. Throw a few acorns, pile up rocks to keep them down, they will force up their way and wedge open the rocks. You cannot hold down a seed with the life germ in it. So Paul's little group of converts by the power of the Holy Spirit grew and flourished and rejoiced in the Lord. They would seem even to have spread the gospel in the districts around. The best modern parallel I know is that of the poor heathen of Uganda, in Africa, whose bishop has told us how they started little missionary bands to carry God's good news to the heathen around them.

The Thessalonians show the quickest growth of any church we know. Only a couple of months later Paul wrote his first epistle to them in great delight. Two months ago they were degraded idolators, he says, who turned from idols to serve the living God. Now already " the word of the Lord hath sounded forth from you in Macedonia and Achaia. In every place your faith towards God has gone forth."

Let us believe more in the power of that living seed. Let us put more heart and hope into our missionary efforts, for we are sowing the seed of eternal life and nothing can stop it. It has the life in itself.

III

I just notice, in passing, his next station, Berea, because it is the only place where the whole synagogue of the Jews gave him a fair hearing. They were not bigots like the other Jews ; and like many of ourselves. They were fair, honest men who could listen with open mind. That is all God wants for His truth. Not blind credulity, but the honest heart that will listen fairly. So the Bereans have come down to us in history with a fine reputation. " These were more noble than those of Thessalonica, for they heard the word with all readiness of mind and searched the Scriptures whether these things were so." They searched the Scriptures, " therefore many of them believed."

We have little more to tell of them. For the bigots

of Thessalonica found out where Paul was and soon Berea b .came too hot to hold him. Paul was the chief object of their pursuit. If they could get rid of him, the others did not matter much. Paul was not very good at taking care of himself. I think he was sick again. The kindly Bereans had to carry him off to the sea and put him on board a ship of the Athens line, but he left Silas and Timothy at Berea to see the little church on its feet, as he had previously left Luke at Philippi. For Paul was not a mere wandering preacher, he was an Apostle and Bishop founding the church. He had to leave everywhere the nucleus of a church with its ordained ministry and sacraments.

I am the more convinced that he must have been sick, for they not only carried him off to the ship, but in the kindness of their hearts they would not let their poor nerve-racked friend go on alone. They went with him and looked after him on the way to Athens and came back with the ship on its return voyage.

IV

Nothing like a sea voyage for a man sick and tired. For three days he is sailing by that lovely coast amid scenes vivid with heroic memories. Poetry and history and romance are on every side. Olympus and Marathon and the pass of Thermopylæ where the Spartans died. And the soft sea breezes are around him bringing God's healing power to body and spirit, till, on the third morning, the clouds on the far horizon began to take on substance. He makes out headlands and cliffs, and then the sun brightens on the distant fairyland of white towers and spires like a delicate lacework against the blue.   That is Athens !   Famous, glorious, beautiful Athens, the world centre of knowledge and beauty and art.

But that is only our point of view.   We should be enthusiastic over Athens.   Paul would not.   His Hebrew ideal was not beauty and art, but Righteousness.   He would value more a sweating slave boy who loved the Lord than a whole university of artists and philosophers.   Some would call this fanaticism.   It depends on their viewpoint.   His passionate missionary zeal seems fanaticism to men who care only for money-making.   His longing after God and his deep sense of sin seem fanaticism to the careless crowd.   It depends on one's viewpoint.   At any rate, like many men who have accomplished great things for the world, he was a man of one persistent idea.

He would feel quite lonely amongst these cultured pagans with no Christian soul to talk with him about Jesus.   He writes touchingly to Thessalonica, " I was left in Athens *alone*."   He directs his Berean friends as they bid him good-bye, " Tell Silas and Timothy to come to me as soon as they can."   A strange city is a lonely place anyway.   A strange pagan city is especially lonely for Paul.

v

I see him next day wandering lonely through that lovely city, wondering at its glorious sights, its stately civic buildings, its splendid temples of Juno and Ceres, and Apollo and Minerva, the multitude of exquisite statues of the gods in gold and silver and white marble.   Every street corner has its deity, every institution has its patron god. One heathen writer tells us that Athens was swarming with statues—another says satirically that it was easier to find gods there than men. If the outward appearance represented inward realities, Athens should be the most religious city in the world.

But, alas, Paul knew that they represented no realities except the shameful realities of impurity and insincerity. Once in early virile days the Greeks were men of purpose. They believed in the supernatural. They believed in the gods, and in the strength of that belief they did heroic deeds which the world will not easily forget.

Now they had lost their faith. The beautiful gods of Olympus were but heroes of fable. Their worship was but a screen for lust and rottenness. Life was beautiful, bright, sparkling, on the surface. But it was utterly hollow. The human soul made in the likeness of God could not get satisfaction out of beauty alone. The day of sorrow came to them and there was no comfort. The day of death came and they had no hope. In art and culture they were first of the nations. If it were possible for human wisdom alone to find out God, Athens must have found him. But, alas, as Paul writes later to the Romans, " the world by wisdom found not God." For it is through spiritual aspiration, not through intellectual knowledge, that men find the Father.

To a cultured tourist Athens of that day would be a dream of beauty and delight. But Paul was not enjoying it. " His spirit was stirred within him as he saw the city crowded with idols." " The ugly little Jew," says Renan, " had no taste for beauty."

That may be. But that is not the explanation. That ugly little Jew stood on a higher plane. His eyes were on God and Righteousness, and the love of Christ, and the strength to conquer sin, and the glory of the life eternal. So he looked on these proud people, not with envy or admiration, but with heartfelt pity. Vanity of vanities. They had missed the Highest.

And the saddest thing was that they were not sad about it at all. People can get accustomed to doing without God. In our own city, as well as in Athens, there are many who seem to get on very well without Him, except in their better moments, when Conscience stirs, when vague aspirations after better things come, when bereavement and sorrow and dissatisfaction with life, bring blind longing for something they hardly know what. At other times—and that is the tragedy of it—they do not miss God at all. That is the tragedy. " Thou sayest I am rich, I have need of nothing, and knowest not that thou art poor and miserable and blind and naked." The Athenians would be amused at the pity of that ugly little Jew. But the ugly little Jew was right.

VI

Wandering amongst this profusion of images, with his spirit stirred within him at a whole city given to idolatry, I see him suddenly pause. I see his attention caught. It is a white statue at a street corner with this inscription, *Agnostō Theō*, " To God unknown." Why does that arrest him ? For this reason, I think, if we may judge from the use he made of it later in his speech, that his broad sympathies read in it an expression of the craving of the heathen world for something higher and better than they knew, a blind "groping after God, if haply they might find Him, who, in truth, is not far away from everyone of us." The early legends of many races bear witness to this craving—from that Arabian idolator before Mahomet's day, repeating his poor prayer, "God, if I knew how Thou wishest to be served, I would serve Thee, but, alas, I know not," to the prayer to the blue sky in the ancient books of India.

> When we tremble like the cloud driven by the wind,
> When we commit an offence through forgetting the right,
> Have mercy, Varuna, have mercy.

These were cries to the unknown God. It was some comfort to Paul in the midst of his despondency. "They have cravings for something beyond what they know. I can at any rate tell them about the unknown God."

VII

So he made it his custom to sit in the stately central square, where the gay idlers met and chatted and gossiped in the afternoon. They were a gay, frivolous, gossiping crowd. Demosthenes had charged their ancestors fiercely, "Instead of guarding your liberties, you are for ever gadding about and looking for news." The Bible story tells us that "they spent their time in nothing else but to tell or to hear some new thing." So they soon got to talking with the ugly Jew. I do not think he was an easy man to talk to, but in this case he wanted to talk, and anybody could get

on with these pleasant and courteous Athenians. So
Paul talked with them, as Socrates four hundred years
earlier had talked, about the unknown God. He
had three or four weeks of this intercourse, and I
cannot help thinking that it accomplished far more
than his famous later speech before the Areopagus.

Soon the philosophers were introduced to him.
Philosophers were thoughtful men, guessing at the riddle
of the universe, and from their conclusions forming
rules of life. They professed to be seekers after truth,
and no man can be that without helping towards
Righteousness. But, of course, their practice often fell
below their professions. The two schools here mentioned are the Epicureans and Stoics. The Epicureans
taught that the world was made by chance. The gods
were not troubling themselves about men. Therefore,
men need not trouble about them. Happiness is the
chief end of man. Therefore, seek happiness. In
theory they would say seek other men's happiness too.
But in degraded days it read : " Seek your own happiness. You will be a short time alive, you will be a
long time dead. Let us eat and drink, for to-morrow
we die."

The Stoic had a nobler teaching. Seek virtue.
Listen to the voice of conscience. Probably there is
some great Being behind that voice. Nobody knows.
But even if not, you should follow the inner voice.
Take life calmly. Do not get excited over it. Bear
its ills silently with dignity. If they get too bad you
can always get out by suicide. With the exception of
the suicide the Stoics had a very noble philosophy of
life. But, of course, they also were not as good as
their creed.

I do not suppose Paul took much interest in their creeds. He was too greatly in earnest about his wonderful gospel. So they were puzzled. Some said he was a mere babbler. Others that he was a setter forth of strange gods because he talked of Jesus and the Resurrection. At any rate, he had something to say which they had not heard before, and they thought his teaching of sufficient importance to be submitted to public inquiry.

VIII

It is the court day of the Areopagus, the Senate which had charge of matters connected with the State religion. On the hill of Mars, beneath the open sky, the councillors are assembled—grave seniors, men of distinction in the nation. Four hundred years before on that same hill the Council had met to judge the greatest of all their thinkers. He was charged with disparaging the gods and bidding men turn to the guiding voice within. And for that Socrates had to drink the hemlock poison. Now they have Paul on a similar charge. But Paul will not have to drink hemlock poison. The Athenians do not take religion so seriously now. They are just politely interested. " May we know what this new teaching is ? " It does not read as if they cared very much. But Paul cared. It was the chance of his life for bringing his message before the cultured scholars and leaders of Greece. He never had an audience like that before and never would again. You may be sure he prepared his speech carefully. You may be sure he prayed hard for the help of the Holy Ghost.

Read the speech over carefully. Let me first offer these preliminary remarks :

(1) Notice how different his sermons to Jews and pagans. With the one he appeals to the Word of God. With the other to the works of God in nature around.

(2) The speech you have here could be said in two minutes, so that evidently it is only a brief summary—perhaps Paul's notes of the speech which he handed to Luke.

(3) The important part was never delivered. Just as he was leading up to his teaching about Christ the audience contemptuously broke up the meeting.

(4) Our version uses an unfortunate word at the opening. " Men of Athens, I perceive that you are too superstitious." Paul would never have said that. Not only would it be discourteous, but it would prejudice his whole speech. The Greek word means religious, devoted to the worship of gods. He used it as a complimentary introduction.

IX

Now hear the speech. Put yourselves in their place. I am Paul. You are the learned and dignified assembly before whom I plead—not for myself, but for my dear Lord. Above us is the open sky. Around us are the glorious temples and the beautiful images gleaming in white marble, and silver and gold. Let me expand the speech as I think he did.

" O Athenians, I perceive that you are a very religious people, devoted to the worship of your gods. You charge me with introducing strange gods. Nay. For as I studied the object of your worship through the city, I came on an altar with this inscription

'To the God unknown.' That unknown God whom you worship, not knowing Him, Him declare I unto you. That unknown God has revealed Himself. He is the one God over all gods who made the world and all things therein. He being Lord of the Earth dwelleth not in temples made with hands as you represent Him. He fills this glorious world around you and all the worlds. It is He who giveth to all life and breath and all things. He has made all the nations and appointed the bounds of their habitations. He has placed them for His gracious purpose that they should seek God if happily they might find Him, who, in truth, is not far from any of us. Deep in your hearts you know this is true. Your own poets confess it. ' We are also his offspring.' "

Up to this, the audience are entirely with him. It is a fine speech and appeals to them.

"Forasmuch as He is so great, and we are His children, we ought not to belittle Him, we ought not to think that the Godhead is like unto these images of gold, silver and stone, graven by art and men's device. Those small thoughts were allowable in the child races of the world. We are beyond that now. The times of the old ignorance God overlooked. But the end of it has come. The race is to rise. Old things are passed away. God has revealed Himself. And now He commandeth every man to repent and turn to Him. For He has revealed Himself, by Him whom He hath ordained who shall one day judge the world. I and my nation have seen the Appointed One. We did not know Him. We crucified Him. But God has given confirmation unto all men in that He hath raised Him from the dead."

X

Now there is coming the crisis of the whole speech, which the rest only led up to. Paul is now going to preach Christ. But in a moment the whole life goes out of his speech. The audience is laughing ! An eager speaker can stand uproar and opposition, but he cannot go on when people are laughing. They are moving in their seats, impatiently muttering to each other, " Nonsense, come away. The man is a fool. Resurrection from the dead, indeed ! Let us get away out of this ! " The chiefs of the assembly are courteous to the end. They bow him politely out of the court. " Thank you, sir, for your speech. We hope to hear you again some other time."

Thus " Paul went out from among them." I see him walk back to his lodging, sore and disappointed, and feeling as every impassioned speaker at such times would feel. " I have failed badly. I might have done better if I had kept back the mention of the Resurrection till I had told them the story of Jesus. Anyway, I am done with these conceited scholars. I go back to the simple work-people who will listen to me. In future I will preach Christ only."

He could not easily forget that day. I see the memory of it repeatedly in his letters later. " Not many wise or noble are called. The wisdom of this world is foolishness with God. We preach Christ crucified to the Jews, a stumbling-block to the Greeks' foolishness—but to us who are called, Christ the power of God and the wisdom of God."

CHAPTER X

THE NEW TESTAMENT IN THE MAKING

PAUL has left Athens, disappointed and discouraged. He has failed—and he does not like failing. And he is a good deal troubled, too, about his converts at Salonika. The last he had seen of them was in the street riot when the Jews had stirred up the scum of the town against them. With keen sympathy he realises all that they have to face, the movements against their faith ; the lies and slanders, the many temptations that would drag them back to their old evil life.

And he can get no news. At Athens, Timothy had caught him up, but in spite of his loneliness, he had sent him to Salonika to help and to report. But no message has come yet.

So Paul is troubled. It is not strange that Paul should have his despondent moments. We are all creatures of temperament. He was a truly happy man. His high faith in God taught him a boundless optimism. He could sing psalms in the dungeon. He could bid his people rejoice always. Neither life nor death had any terrors for a man who knew God as he did. Every Christian has a right to go through life with this optimist attitude.

But we all have our passing fits of depression,

especially if we are in bad health, when we are not able to realise all that we have to be glad about. I don't suppose they do us much harm, provided that they come seldom. It is human, and Paul was very human.

II

So it was a rather troubled man that walked one day unnoticed and unknown into the great, wealthy, wicked city of Corinth. How little the people of Corinth could have imagined that in ages to come the chief historic significance of their great city would centre on the fact that this poor Jewish missionary had come that day into it. Down in the lower town he finds a tent-maker at his shop door. He asks for work. The tent-maker is a friendly man, and takes rather a fancy to him. He tells him that his name is Aquila, lately banished with other Jews from Rome. He introduces him to his good wife Priscilla, and gives him a place in the workshop and a room in his house. And thus begins one of the pleasantest friendships of Paul's life, a friendship that resulted for Aquila and Priscilla in the joy of becoming followers of Christ.

Thus Paul began his ministry in Corinth, " in weakness and fear and much trembling," he says. His failure in Athens had evidently shaken him. I think he expected to fail in Corinth too. One hardly wonders. For Corinth was about the most wicked city of the world at the time. Its vice was so rampant and unblushing that it became a proverb. " A Corinthian drinker," a " Corinthian banquet," were bywords for the lowest profligacy.

But he must face it. Every day he worked in the

shop, and you may be sure that workshop was a purer, nobler place for his presence. Would that that could be said of us all! Every evening, after work was done, he tried to tell people about Jesus, and the conquering power of the Holy Ghost over sin. And every Sabbath he reasoned in the synagogue. But the Jews had little sympathy with him. They could not stand his teaching, that all the proud hopes of their nation for centuries had ended in a Messiah on the cross of shame. At last they rose up fiercely against him, contradicting and blaspheming.

There was a limit to what Paul could stand from them. One day in fierce anger he shook out his raiment in stern repudiation. " Your blood be on your own heads, henceforth I go to the Gentiles." Then the fight was on. Paul did not shirk it. He hired a little hall next door. He drew crowds of people. He converted and baptised Crispus, their chief in the synagogue. There could be no truce with him after that.

It was not a pleasant time. But he could bring all his troubles and leave them with God. And every night he could talk things over with Aquila and Priscilla. And then, one night when things were at their worst, came the turn of the tide. The Lord appeared unto him in the visions of the night, " Fear not, Paul, and hold not thy peace, For I am with thee, I have much people in this city." In a moment the whole outlook changed. The sun was shining, the world was bright. What mattered anything with Christ beside him, and the power of the Omnipotent at his back ! It was a changed man that his friends saw at breakfast next morning.

III

Thus began one of the most successful missions of his life. Perhaps it was because his preaching had grown simpler and more intense. There was a rebound from his philosophical preaching which had failed at Athens.

Now he would talk only about Christ. He writes later to these Corinthians, who had compared his teachings with the clever oratory of Apollos: " I was determined to know nothing among you save Jesus Christ, and Him crucified." As a result many believed and were baptised. We learn from his Corinthian letters what sort of people they were. " Not many wise nor noble," mostly working people, and many of the profligate and degraded classes. Corinth was a city of drunkards, extortioners and libertines. He tells them straight out. " Neither fornicators nor adulterers, nor effeminate, nor abusers of themselves with mankind, nor thieves, nor covetous, nor extortioners shall inherit the Kingdom of God, *and such were some of you.*" These were the people on whom to test the power of Christianity. If Christ could save them from sin, He could save anybody. And He plainly was saving them. Men could see it in the bright, hopeful faces, marked deep with lines of debauchery and sin. Grafters and drunkards and thieves and jail birds and prostitutes were mingled in that little meeting-room with people of decent lives. But they all had the peace of God in their hearts, and the light of hope in their eyes. They had tested Christ and He had not failed them. Religion becomes an intensely real and practical thing when men see results like that. If you were Paul and had a gospel that could do that, would you not feel that nothing was too much to do for it ? You are not Paul. But you have a gospel like that. Don't you forget it in your missionary efforts.

So came hope and courage back to Paul, and he wondered why he had ever been so despondent.

IV

Then something else very pleasant happened. One day a shadow falls through the door of the workshop ; he looks up from his tent-making to see Silas and Timothy standing at the door ! News at last from Salonika ! And it is delightful news that Timothy brings. " They are unshaken in the faith. They are making fine progress. The heathen are impressed by them. And they have the kindliest feelings for you, Paul. They are most affectionate about you, and are longing to see you again." It was a great delight to Paul. " I live again," he says, " when ye stand fast in the Lord."

" Of course," Timothy said, " it is not all rose-coloured. Some have fallen back. A. and B. and the old sailorman C. have been drinking badly. Those three girls near the city gate have gone back on the street. And there is another thing I do not like. There is a rather unwholesome excitement about the second coming of Christ that keeps the people restless and disinclined for quiet work. And death has been busy with the little congregation. Our old friend on the hill has lost his wife. Four of our men were drowned at Cenchrea last month, and the mourners are not only sorrowing for their dear ones, but rather perplexed as well. They are asking, What about the second coming of the Lord in our lifetime. Our beloved are dead. Have they missed him altogether? And so on."

I see Timothy telling the news. I watch the eagerness of Paul, and the quick changes on his face as he listens.

" O, Timothy, I wish I could go to them this moment. But I cannot, with this growing congregation so eager in Corinth. Look here, go down to the artist's shop in the next street and buy sheets of papyrus. We will write them a letter."

That was a happy thought for the world. Thus began the most important stage in Paul's great life work. Thus began the making of the New Testament.

v

Perhaps you do not all know that the New Testament began with the writing of the Epistles. And that Paul began it that day in the shabby little workshop of Aquila, the tent-maker.

It is the year 50 A.D., 17 years after the Crucifixion. There was no Bible except the Old Testament. Not a page of our gospels was written yet—nor for nearly twenty years afterwards. It is a curious fact. One would have expected that the first thing Christians would do after Pentecost would be to go to the Apostles and ask them, Write us down in a book at once everything that you have seen and heard and learned about Jesus in those wonderful three years. But they did not. You see, they were not accustomed to books.

They did not want books. Most of them could not read. Their whole training had been oral. Their knowledge of a thing had always come by hearsay. There were no newspapers. When there was any news somebody told it. Written books or read books, except the Bible, were not at all in their line.

They were simple, plain people, fishers and farmers and servants and tent-makers and artisans. They were very happy in their new religion. One thought dominates all life for them. "We know that the Son of God is come." They want to hear everything about Him. But they do not want books.

Also, if you put yourself in their place, you will see that it is hardly worth while writing books. For, mingled with their new joy, is a restless expectancy. They believe that Jesus will come back during their lifetime to take them all to Heaven. They do not know the moment. It may be any day, " at evening or at midnight, or at cockcrow or in the morning." Even Paul expects this. He writes in this very Epistle to the Thessalonians, " We which are alive and remain unto the coming of the Lord." So with Heaven lying about them there was no need of writing books for the future. There was no future except a future in glory with the Lord.

So they gathered together in their weekly assemblies to listen to the burning words of men who had been with Jesus or had learned about Him from those who had. The prominent facts were most frequently taught, the Incarnation, the Crucifixion, the Resurrection, the Ascension, the Glorified Jesus.

And everywhere in a hundred places together were the preparation classes for Baptism like our

Confirmation classes. Converts had to be taught in regular order the life of Jesus. They grew quite familiar with it.

Thus there arose an ORAL GOSPEL published through the whole Church, not in written books, but in the fleshly tables of the heart. By and by the listeners wrote out little bits of it, Sayings of Jesus and such like. But not one of our four gospels were written till nearly twenty years after this date.

VI

So the first Christian writings were the Epistles of St. Paul, and first of them all was this letter to the Thessalonians, called forth by the simple necessities of the moment. God's ways are not our ways. We should probably expect the Christian Bible to begin with solemn, formal, logically written books. But God knows best. We believe that the Holy Ghost was inspiring Paul. And we believe that He guided him to write not formal treatises, but simple, natural, unconventional letters, such as we should write ourselves to-day to our soldier boys in this same Salonika. A formal treatise might have its advantages. But this simple letter style had its advantages too. It was more natural. It gave more scope for freedom of expression and intensity of feeling and the free familiarity of personal intercourse.

Paul wrote straight from the heart. This gives that vivid freshness of style, that intenseness and sincerity and personal touch. A formal book would never have moved the world as these letters have done. Take away the traces of passion, the stern denunciation, the affectionate entreaties, the frank colloquialism, the personal details, and you would never have had the grip of these writings on the soul of the world. God guided Paul to write simple, natural letters, and when you read them you had better keep that in mind.

Thessalonians is Paul's first Epistle. I wish some publishers would have the courage of breaking with the stupid old tradition and print the Bible with the Epistles in their chronological order. It would help us to understand the development of Paul's thought, and in some measure, the development of the early Church. The present arrangements seems to be based on no plan, or on the plan of putting the longest first and then arranging in order of length. We have actually Paul's first Epistles and his last side by side. It is very stupid. But it has gone on so long that people are afraid to change it. I am in correspondence with a great Bible house, and I am hoping to persuade them to try a small edition of the Bible printed in the way I suggest. It will need some courage. But it will have valuable results if they do it.

VII

Now I picture to myself the very first beginning in the making of the New Testament. Paul and Silas and Timothy are in the shabby workshop after hours. They have bought the papyrus sheets in the artist's shop around the corner. Parchment was not used for letters. In any case it would be too dear for poor people. But they could buy papyrus sheets in the shops as we buy foolscap from six to eighteen inches wide and of any length required. We know that from the papyri that have been discovered.

Paul is dictating the letter while he works. Busy people then, as now, dictated when they could, instead of writing, and perhaps Paul's weak eyes made it more necessary in his case. At any rate, we know that it was his custom. Then at the close he would scrawl in a few words of blessing or remembrance with his name, " which is my token," he says, " in every epistle." This dictation gives much of the vividness in his letters, the broken sentences, the frequent interruptions of his thought.

They are just his rapid thoughts taken down as they arise. I think Silas is the writer, for I find him afterwards acting as writer in the epistle of Peter (1 Peter, v. 12). Now listen to Paul dictating :

" Paul and Silvanus "—(Silas is short for Silvanus, but Paul is a dignified person and calls men by their full names). " Paul and Silvanus and Timothy to the Church of the Thessalonians, grace be to you and peace."

" But," I hear Silas say, " Paul, this is your letter —our names should not appear."

" No, Silvanus, it is our letter. We feel the same about our friends in Thessalonika."

I like to think of the kindliness, and modesty, and generous courtesy of the man associating his subordinates as equals with himself. And I think, too, how little these two thought that day that they were writing in that mean little workroom the first words of the great Christian Scriptures for all ages to come.

VIII

First, he must let them know how glad he is:

We give thanks to God always for you all, making mention of you in our prayers; remembering without ceasing your work of faith and labour of love and patience of hope in our Lord Jesus Christ, before our God and Father.

Then he changes the note. He is thinking of all the slanders of his enemies about him, that he was not a real apostle like the others, that he had some self-seeking purpose, that this collecting of money for the poor looked suspicious, etc. "You know it is not true," he says.

"God is my witness that I did not hide covetousness under fair pretences . . . that I did not seek anything from you. You remember how I worked night and day that I might not burden any of you, while I proclaimed the glad tidings of God."

"I am longing to see you again. I tried to get to you, but I could not. I have been very anxious about you. When I was left in Athens alone, I sent Timothy to inquire about you. He has only just come back with the happy news, and I am greatly comforted. For I live again if ye be steadfast in the Lord."

"And now I want to write about your manner of life. Watch especially against lustful passions, the chief sin of your past life and your great danger still. For God hath not called us to uncleanness, but unto holiness."

"Concerning brotherly love I need not write to you, for you are taught of God to love one another. But I desire that you settle down quietly to work. Do not get restless and excited about the coming of the Lord. He may come any day. I know not when, but let Him find you doing your ordinary work well, that the outsiders may not reproach us."

Then comes his tender thought of them mourning for their dead, and troubled because their dear ones have missed the second coming. With deep sympathy he dictates that classic passage, the comfort of countless mourners in all the ages since.

I would not have you to be ignorant brethren concerning them that are asleep, that ye sorrow not even as others which have no hope.

For if we believe that Jesus died and rose again, so also those that sleep in Jesus will God bring with Him. For this we say unto you by the word of the Lord, that we which are alive and remain unto the coming of the Lord shall not go before those who are asleep.

For the Lord Himself shall descend from Heaven with the voice of the archangel and the trump of God. And the dead in Christ shall rise first. Then we who remain shall be caught up with them to meet the Lord in the air, wherefore comfort one another with these words.

Next comes a little set of short practical exhortations.

Rejoice evermore. Pray without ceasing. Continue to give thanks whatever be your lot. Quench not the spirit. Keep clear of every form of evil.

Now I see him scrawling in the conclusion of the letter himself in his own handwriting.

May the God of peace sanctify you wholly, and may your spirit and soul and body be preserved blameless at the offering of Our Lord Jesus Christ. God will fulfil my prayer for you. And brethren, pray ye for me. See that this letter be read to all the brethren. The grace of Our Lord Jesus Christ be with you.

I wish you would read that letter through at one sitting. You can do it in fifteen minutes. And as you read it, call up in your mind that poor tent-maker

E

dictating it with the joy of God in his heart, and the tender, solicitous sympathy for the friends he loved. Put yourself in his place. Put life and heart into it. Make it real.

IX

A few months later he writes again. I shall not comment on the second Epistle. It is not nearly as interesting as the first. Evidently he has heard that they are losing balance, in their restless excitement expecting Christ any day. They will not settle down to ordinary work, but are going about in dreamy contemplation, singing and holding prayer meetings and watching for the Lord.

History tells of a similar condition more than once. In the year 1000 A.D., and at the time of the Reformation, and more or less at other times, even down to fifty years ago, when fanatics were prophesying and fixing dates for the end of the world. We had a slight renewal of it recently, owing to the war.

This letter is written to steady the Thessalonians. Its main thought is expressed in that old story of New England, when one day in one of those times of excitement about the end of the world, a sudden darkness came at noonday while the Assembly was in sitting. Men got frightened and cried, " It is the coming of Christ, it is the end of the world."

" Bring in candles," said the old president, " and go on with your work. If the Lord is coming, how better can He find us than quietly doing our duty."

That is the spirit of Paul's second Epistle to the Thessalonians

CHAPTER XI

DIANA OF THE EPHESIANS.

AFTER writing the Thessalonian letters Paul remained on in Corinth, founding a Church of Christ amongst the lowest classes, largely slaves and people of degraded life. On the one hand, it was the most inspiring work, proving the glorious power of Christ on the lowest sinners. But on the other hand, as we see later, such classes make a perilous setting for a church unless their founder can stay with them. Perhaps that was why he stayed nearly two years.

But he must go on. He is the pioneer of the gospel to the civilised world. He cannot stay in one place. He can only ordain presbyters and instruct them carefully and entrust Corinth to his Lord.

So early in the year 53 A.D. he starts for Jerusalem to keep the Passover, and then steers straight for his home base at Antioch, the city of the Colonnades, from which he had started five years ago on his second missionary journey. There is not time to follow him here. You must imagine for yourselves the interest of his Passover at Jerusalem, meeting the other Apostles, telling of his work, mingling in the worshipping crowd from every land. I do not think he enjoyed it as much as we should expect. He was never very happy with the Jerusalem Christians. They were timid, conservative, bigoted. They looked askance at his daring revolutionary methods with the heathen. It is pleasanter to picture his triumphant reception at the dear old home church of Antioch, now become the great mother church of Gentile Christianity. He was their beloved chief and hero. He belonged especially to them. Theirs was the high honour of having sent him forth on his already famous world mission for their Lord.

How delightful if he could stay with them ! But he must not. The vastness of his life work is being revealed to him. And old age is coming in sight. Not many years left, and so much to do before the end. So he bids good-bye to his beloved Antioch, never to see it again, and starts on the greatest and most fruitful stage of his life, which was to end at the headsman's block in Rome.

II

First came his episcopal visitation as we may call it, confirming many churches which he had founded, passing through his boyhood home at Tarsus, visiting Lystra, the home of his young comrade Timothy. I cannot follow him in this journey. At its close I present him entering the great city of Ephesus to claim its surrender to the Kingdom of Christ. So far as we can judge, Timothy was with him, and also another young comrade, Titus, who now comes prominently into his life. And who do you think were waiting for him in that lonely heathen city ? His dear old friends from Corinth, Aquila and Priscilla, of the tent-maker's shop! You can imagine what it meant to a lonely, burdened man to find that kindly old couple waiting to receive him.

It was most important for the Church to get a footing in Ephesus, a great central city, with its fine Roman roads branching out in every direction. In its district lay the six towns whose names are so familiar now through the Book of the Revelation of St. John, Sardis and Smyrna and Philadelphia and Laodicea and Pergamos and Thyatira, the city of Lydia the seller of purple. St. John, you know, in his later life settled down as Bishop of Ephesus, so you will understand why these churches were in his mind as he wrote " to the angel of the church in Sardis," " to the angel of the church in Thyatira," and so on. These, with Ephesus, are the seven churches, founded most probably during this mission by Paul and his companions. Ephesus has a high claim on our attention, if only for these churches. And Ephesus has a still higher claim on our attention as giving us fifty years later the Gospel of St. John. Pity someone could not tell to Paul on that lonely day of his entry, what Ephesus would afterwards mean to the Church of God.

It did not look much like it that day. Ephesus was one of the greatest strongholds of paganism Its fame rested chiefly on its magnificent temple of Diana, one of the seven wonders of the world. The sun, it was said, saw nothing in his course more glorious than the temple of Diana at Ephesus. The whole province of Asia contributed to its erection. All the Greek cities around were enthusiastic about it. It was the great rallying point of heathenism. You can see it depicted on the Ephesian coins in the British Museum to-day with its ugly black idol that fell down from Jupiter. The Ephesians were inordinately proud of their black idol and of the fame of their city as the temple-keeper of Diana.

This worship of Diana made Ephesus the centre of magic and sorcery. There the professors of the black art practised their incantations openly. They could raise the devil, they could frighten the wits—and the money—out of their credulous votaries, calling up evil spirits, principalities and powers and rulers of darkness. You remember how Paul thinks of it in his letter to these Ephesians. " We wrestle not with flesh and blood but against principalities and powers, and the rulers of darkness and the spiritual hosts of wickedness in high places."

Think of a poor missionary facing that abode of Satan with nothing but his improbable little story of Jesus and his little service of Bread and Wine—to win for his Lord a vast pagan city of half a million souls ! Surely Christ must have been very real to him when he could dare to attempt such an enterprise as that. Surely Paul, if he were not the wildest of dreamers, must have had a tremendous faith in the presence and power of the Eternal Son of God. If we had even a tithe of his faith to-day we, too, should turn the world upside down in our enthusiasm. That Son of God is just as real and as close and as powerful to-day. But, alas ! we do not turn the world upside down for Him. Fools that we are, and slow of heart to believe ! Lord increase our faith !

III

At the very beginning of his mission in Ephesus we get a curious sidelight on the story. He met one day twelve men. They seemed to be baptised Christians, but they rather puzzled him, their ideas were so defective. He asked them, " Have ye received the Holy Ghost when ye believed ? " The gift of the Holy Ghost, you know, was conferred by laying on of apostolic hands after baptism. The whole Catholic church continues this still in the rite of Confirmation. So that Paul's question would mean as if we should ask, Have ye been confirmed since ye believed ? Have ye received the Holy Ghost by the laying on of hands after baptism ? " No," they said, " we have not so much as heard about the Holy Ghost." " Into what then were ye baptised ? " And they said, " Into John's baptism." So he discovered the curious fact that they were disciples of John the Baptist's teaching, and had never got any farther. Then he taught them the fuller teaching about Christ, and the gift of the Holy Ghost, and handed them over to his assistants to be baptised, and then he laid his hands on them, and the power of the Holy Ghost fell on them.

That was an interesting experience for Paul. But it was doubly so when Aquila and Priscilla got talking with him about things that had happened in his absence. They told him of another man of the same group, a great scholar and most attractive preacher, mighty in the Scriptures. His name was Apollos. His preaching had made quite a sensation in Ephesus before Paul came. In spite of his defective teaching,

he was like another Baptist preparing the way of the
Lord. Aquila and Priscilla went one day to hear him.
It was powerful preaching, but they missed the confident ring of Paul. They saw that the preacher did not
know what they knew. So they made friends with him
—I think anybody would make friends with that dear
old couple—and he came often to their house, and they
taught him the way of God fully as they had learned
it from Paul. And now he was off in Corinth preaching
Jesus Christ.

Was not it nice to hear that? Those dear old
friends could not preach, but they could love and
make religion lovable, and they could tell in simple
words about the Lord who was so dear to them. I
think you would enjoy knowing Aquila and Priscilla.

By the way, there was some trouble about this
matter later on in Corinth. For Apollos was a much
more attractive and eloquent preacher than Paul.
And like some modern Christians, some of the
Corinthians ran after their favourite preacher, and
boasted about his superiority over Paul. We shall
hear of this later on.

IV

As usual, Paul began with the Synagogue of the
Jews, and, as usual, the Jews cast him out. They
could not stand the shame of a crucified Messiah.
It is one of the mysterious tragedies of history, that
rejection of the Messiah by His own people who had
been looking forward to Him for 1,000 years. As St.
John pathetically puts it, " He came unto His own
and His own received Him not."

Then a lecturer named Tyrannus lent his school after hours, and there for two whole years, as he tells afterwards, he ceased not to admonish everyone day and night with tears, preaching both to Jews and Greeks, " repentance toward God and faith toward Our Lord Jesus Christ." The same simple old Gospel which the Church has to teach to-day. Very practical. Very simple. No cleverness required to understand it. " The wayfaring men, though fools, shall not err therein." Just that I should see my sin and be sorry for it, and turn to God with earnest resolve—and then —just trust myself utterly to Christ.

v

Through the blessing of Him who was watching over Paul, that simple Gospel became a mighty power in Ephesus, in the midst of its foul sins and idolatries and black magic. I read that not only the Ephesians, but the whole province of Asia heard the word of the Lord Jesus, both Jews and Greeks. I read that the Church grew so fast that it needed many presbyters to preside over it.* I read of one never-to-be-forgotten scene where, in the midst of an enthusiastic crowd, the professors of sorcery and magic brought their cabalistic books into the square for a great bonfire, and while the books were burning, and the Christians were praising God, some one calculated roughly the value of those books at 50,000 pieces of silver. It was like the days of Savonarola at Florence in the Middle Ages. You can imagine the delight of

* Acts xx.: 17.

Paul as he watched that fire, and thanked God for the honest practical religion which caused it, and for the glorious triumph of his dear Lord in Ephesus.

VI

The devil has to get busy at a time like that. So we are not surprised at another spectacular event soon after. It is the month of May, the month of Diana, when the whole province has crowded into Ephesus for the annual celebrations. From the towns of the coast and the interior they swarm, in their picturesque, national dress, to enjoy the games and revelries, in honour of their goddess. It was a brilliant sight. To the Jews it would call up the historic picture of that famous day in Babylon long ago—of Nebuchadnezzar, and Shadrach, Meshach and Abednego, and the image which Nebuchadnezzar the King had set up.

This was the great harvest time for the makers of shrines and images. But this year there is a serious drop in their trade. The Christians have been teaching that " the Godhead is not like to silver and gold graven by art and men's device." The bonfire in the square has set people thinking. The craft of the image makers is in serious danger.

So, in the midst of the gay celebrations, Demetrius the silversmith calls the craftsmen together to lecture them—on religion. Demetrius was very much concerned about the injury to religion—when it touched his pocket. That is a very human touch. When the tariff injures the trade in cattle, the farmer writes letters about the danger to the country. When the drink trade is injured by prohibition, we hear stirring appeals for the liberty of the subject. So Demetrius is greatly troubled " lest the image of the great goddess Diana should be despised, whom all Asia and the world worshippeth."

Soon the mob has caught up the cry, and a rush is made for the Jewish quarter and the tent-maker's shop. They are on a visit to Paul. If they had caught Paul just then it would have finished these lectures. But Paul was not at home. Aquila and Priscilla had probably made clever plans. " They risked their necks for me," says Paul in his Roman epistle. At any rate, the mob did not get him. He tried to go and face them when he saw danger for his friends, but the brethren held him back, and the Asiarchs, who presided over the games, sent him a kindly message that his coming would only do worse harm by exciting the mob. So the mob had to spend their energies in shouting through the streets for the space of two hours. " Great is Diana of the Ephesians." There is a capital little touch here about the intelligence of mobs, " the greater part knew not why they were come together."

We believe that Paul and the disciples were praying. We believe that the Lord was watching over His little Church, and could guide the hearts of men, whether pagan or Christian. God works by ordinary means. Two hours of shouting does a good deal to tire people, and the whole mad uproar, which might have had serious results, fizzled out after a wise speech from the town clerk of Ephesus. " Go home and be quiet. If Demetrius and his friends have any cause of complaint, the courts are open to them. As for you, your city is in grave danger of being called in question for this day's uproar."

Though Paul escaped with his life, his letter written from Ephesus at this time hints of a terrible time. "After the manner of men I fought with beasts in Ephesus—despairing even of life—buffeted, reviled, persecuted, defamed, made as the filth of the world and the off-scouring of all things."

He makes very little of these outward things, but in one verse he refers to a burden which we do not sufficiently keep in mind, "that which cometh upon me daily, the care of all the churches." I refer to it now, because it introduces his Epistle to the Corinthians, written at this time from Ephesus.

VII

"The care of all the churches." During all this time of strain he had been watching anxiously over the many churches he had founded. So little would suffice to throw them back. Just now he is especially troubled about his last mission, the young church in Corinth. Disquieting rumours had come. Degraded heathen people do not become saints in a moment. While he was with them, things went well. But that was three years ago. And they were living in very wicked surroundings, where Christian purity and honesty were things to be laughed at, and where everything tended to drag them back into the old evil life. In their first enthusiasm for Christ they thought they could never fall. But Corinth was not Heaven. Christ had not come back. The dull, prosaic life had to be lived, and the Heavenly vision began to fade.

Apollos, the great preacher, had come back to Ephesus, and could tell Paul what was happening in Corinth. So he wrote the Corinthians a letter, which is now lost (see 1 Cor. v., 9), bidding them to cast out fornicators from the Church.

Then they wrote back a self-satisfied, conceited letter which vexed him a good deal. In this letter they asked him several questions. Whether second marriages were lawful to Christians. Whether a Christian should divorce his heathen wife. Whether men should marry at all in view of the coming of Christ. Whether they might eat meats offered to idols. They wanted directions about church services, and especially Holy Communion, and they had serious difficulties, too, about the Resurrection. The letter was not pleasant reading.

Meantime some Christians of the household of Chloe had come and told him still worse things. Nowadays when things go wrong in the Church, we are pointed back to the delightful days of the early Church when everybody was so holy and happy. Paul's experience takes the glamour off this. True, there were many who were a joy to his heart. But to his deep distress he learns that schisms and factions had arisen—that the church worship was often irreverent and disorderly —men had been seen drunk at the Holy Communion— that uncleanness of life was easily tolerated. Indeed, there was one horrible story of a baptised Christian living in open sin with his stepmother in his father's lifetime and the Church had not cast him out, probably because he was rich and important.

Paul was horrified. It was enough to make any man but Paul throw up his work in despair. But Paul was not built that way. It was Christ's work and he trusted Christ. If Christ could have patience with these people just out of heathenism, he must have patience. You may be sure there was much of prayer and deep communion with God before he dictated to Sosthenes that most interesting of all his letters, his first Epistle to the Corinthians. I have but space to touch on a few prominent points, that may help you to read this epistle for yourselves.

VIII

After thanking God for all the good that is still amongst them through the grace of Christ, he goes on

Now I beseech you brethren that there be no divisions amongst you. For it hath been told me by those of Chloe's household that ye are divided. "I am of Paul, I of Apollos, I of Cephas, I of Christ." Is Christ divided? Was Paul crucified for you? Were ye baptised into the name of Paul? What is Apollos and what is Paul? Ministers through whom ye believed. Never think of us. Keep Christ before you. Keep your unity in Christ.

I hear sad things of you. And ye are not ashamed and sorrowful about it. Ye are conceited and puffed up, as though I would not come back with my authority as Christ's apostle. What will ye? Shall I have to come with a rod? I wrote unto you in a former letter, not to keep company with fornicators. And you conceitedly tell me that this is impossible unless you went out of the world altogether. You know what I meant. Now I tell you distinctly—if any baptised Christian be a fornicator, or idolator, or drunkard, cast him out of the Church, banish him, do not even eat with him. A horrible story has come to me of a Christian man living in sin with his father's wife. And ye are not ashamed. Now I command you to gather the Church together, in the name of Our

Lord Jesus Christ, and cast him out for his soul's good. Deliver him to Satan, for the destruction of his flesh, that his spirit may be saved in the day of the Lord.

And here is another wrong. How dare you Christian people bring lawsuits against each other in heathen courts, so that they mock at your religion of love ?

Now, concerning the things you asked me about. First about marriage and the chastity of marriage. These are my directions. (Here comes in a whole chapter of directions. I notice just one point concerning divorce of a heathen wife or husband. Do not do it. Do not marry heathens. But if you are already married do not separate. How do you know that you may not save that heathen wife or husband as they watch your Christian life ?)

That commonsense advice appeals to us all. Paul evidently had not before him the more difficult case that has repeatedly come up in our day in the missions in Africa, where the convert has already half a dozen heathen wives. A Christian cannot live in polygamy. Shall he divorce them all ? Or shall he keep one, and if so, which one ? The first one or the one he likes best ? This question has caused grave perplexity to Archbishops of Canterbury, and I am sure the English bishops have often wished that Paul had had such a case.

Now, concerning meats offered to idols. Since an idol is nothing but a piece of brass it does not really matter. You are free, but take care how you use your freedom. For you have to think of weaker brethren who have not full knowledge. You may do them harm by doing a thing which otherwise is not really wrong. They may think it a justification of idolatry. You must think of them. If even the innocent eating of meat cause my brother to offend, I will eat no meat while the world lasteth lest it make my brother to offend.

That is an important rule for the guidance of the
Christian conscience. It may be an innocent thing
to drink wine. You, perhaps, may do it quite safely,
but you must also consider if your action may do
harm to others who cannot do it safely. For a Christian man who has lovingly worshipped God and
received His Holy Communion, it is quite an innocent
thing to play a game of golf on Sunday. If you
were on a desert island with a couple of Christian
friends I should see no harm in it. But suppose you
do it in this city with a crowd of careless, godless men,
who habitually neglect the worship of God—see
how much harm the example may do. They do not
know your heart or how earnestly you have worshipped
God this morning. They will be encouraged in their
sin. Therefore, you are not always at liberty to do
what is innocent.

Now, concerning the Holy Communion. Think of the awful-
ness of approaching Christ in a drunken condition. For Christ
Himself is in that sacrament. For I have received of the Lord
that which I delivered unto you that the Lord Jesus, the same
night that He was betrayed, took bread and blessed it and
said, " This is My body." In like manner He took this cup
and said, " This is the new covenant in My blood. This do in
remembrance of Me "

The bread which we break is it not the communion of the
Body of Christ.

The cup which we bless is it not the communion of the Blood
of Christ.

Wherefore, whosoever shall eat and drink unworthily is
guilty of the body and blood of the Lord. He eateth and
drinketh judgment to himself not discerning the Lord's body.

Then come other questions to be answered. But
instead of giving petty rules and exact details he lifts

all life up into the presence of his Lord and his Lord's great law of love.

You want rules of spiritual gifts, about precedence in the church, about your relations in the world. I show unto you a more excellent way. Charity suffereth long and is kind ; charity envieth not. Charity vaunteth not itself, is not puffed up, doth not behave itself uncourteously, beareth all things, believeth all things, hopeth all things.

Then comes the magnificent fifteenth chapter at the close, the great Resurrection Lesson of the Church through all the centuries. Death matters little, since Christ is at the other side. " O, Death, where is thy sting ? O, Grave, where is thy victory ? "

I close with the thought how God brings good out of evil. Do you not think it was worth while to have all that evil in the church in Corinth, and all those doubts and questionings and errors, to bring to us those glorious chapters on conscience and charity, and on the Resurrection ?

CHAPTER XII

THE CARE OF ALL THE CHURCHES

THE period dealt with in this chapter, about nine months of the year 56 A.D., is rather difficult and perhaps not very interesting. St. Luke, in his diary, passes it over with a few sentences. We might do the same if we were dealing, as he is, only with Paul's life. But his letters also come into our plan. And his three most important letters were written in this period.

In the last chapter we saw him deeply troubled about his converts in Corinth and writing his most interesting First Epistle to the Corinthians. This he sent by his young comrade Titus. Since then, rumours have come that things were worse than he thought. The bigoted Jerusalem Christians are busy again trying to tie up the great free Gospel in the swaddling clothes of the Jewish Law, and they have many adherents in Corinth.

The Church in Corinth seems in danger of utter disruption. Now he is at Troas impatiently waiting for Titus and for news.

You remember Troas on the historic plains of Troy, whence he started on his mission to Europe

six years before. Then there were only himself and
his three comrades, four Christians in Europe. Now
he can look back on thousands of converts and the
Church in Europe fairly started. He ought to be
in high spirits over it. But he is not. The rumours
from Corinth have shaken him badly. He is very
despondent ; all the more so because he seems to be
sick again of his old humiliating, depressing malady,
" the thorn in the flesh " as he calls it. In the second
Corinthian letter, which I am just coming to, he says,
" I prayed the Lord thrice to relieve me of it, but
the only comfort I got was, ' My grace is sufficient
for thee.' "

II

From Troas he moves to Philippi—to the Jailer
and Lydia and the dear people that he loved best,
I think, of all his converts. And there at last Titus
met him.

" Titus, tell me how they do in Corinth ? Is the
Church in danger ? Have they read my letter ? How
did they take it ? "

Titus tells him, " The majority are loyal. In the
main they took your directions kindly. They have
cast out that incestuous sinner. They are reforming
abuses. I think the loyal churchmen will be quite
able to save the Church."

What a relief for Paul ! " God, who comforteth
the despondent, comforted me by the coming of
Titus."

But Titus adds, " The trouble about doctrine is
still serious. There is a strong minority who are

very bitter. Of course, the Jerusalem crowd are at the back of the trouble, and have seduced some of our people."

" What are they saying ? "

" Oh, just the same old things—that your teaching is dangerous—that you are no real apostle, since you have not been commissioned by Jesus when on earth. They say you are vain and self-seeking—that you are brave in your letters, but cowardly in their presence. In fact, they are taking every mean advantage of your absence. They are even whispering ugly insinuations about money, about this collection of yours for the poor saints at Jerusalem."

Poor Paul ! This was his thanks for all he had done and suffered. Do not forget this when you get little thanks for your efforts.

Fancy all this coming on a man already depressed and sick. Many of us, too, have had our discouraging experiences. Well for us if, like Paul, we can go to Our Lord with them.

All through his letters you see that was where his comfort lay. Jesus was his stand-by. He was a poor, weak, lovably human man, nervous, sleepless, depressed about his troubles. But the calm, strong Son of God was there to flee to. Jesus was not nervous or sleepless or depressed about things. Paul could leave all in His hands who loved him and sympathised. That was the secret of his strength.

III

Paul is thankful for the faithful Christians. But he is uneasy and he is very indignant. He sees the grave danger to the Church. He is not going to stand much more of this. " You go right back, Titus, with another letter."

Thus we get the Second Epistle to the Corinthians. It is quite different from the first. It is intense, strained, passionate. The air is electric. Keen irony, indignation, warning, threatening, bold insistence on his apostolic authority from Christ. It is the Church's danger that has roused him. But through it all you can see the personal note too. You can see that his heart is quivering. For Paul is a very sensitive man, who loves his people and has been hurt to the quick by their desertion. Strong men have often their sensitive nerve spots very near to the surface.

In the first part of the Epistle he seems thinking of the faithful friends. The hurt feeling shews itself. But he does not let himself go till the tenth chapter. There he hits out hard. But he hits out like a gentleman—with the quiet dignity of a Christian man :

Now I, Paul, exhort you by the gentleness of Christ, I who am mean forsooth and contemptible in outward presence yet very bold at a distance. I beseech you don't force me to shew the boldness with which I reckon to deal with some of you when I return. The weapons that I wield are not fleshly weapons, but mighty in God's strength to overthrow adversaries. I am ready to punish all who may be disobedient. I have the authority which the Lord hath given me. I am not writing empty threats. " For his letters," says one, " are weighty and powerful, but in bodily presence and speech he is contemptible." Let such a man assure himself that I will bear out my words by deeds. They boast and commend themselves. They are forsooth the old church, the true Hebrews, the seed of Abraham. But a man is worthy not when he commends himself but when the Lord commends him.

If men are to boast, perhaps I, too, should have something to boast of. I entreat you do not count me a fool. Or if you do, you are such wise people you might bear with a fool and let him boast a little like these very Apostolic people from Jerusalem. Are they Hebrews ? So am I. Are they the seed of Abraham ? So am I. Are they ministers of Christ ? I speak as a fool. I am more. In labours more abundant—in stripes above measure, in prisons more frequent, in deaths oft. Of the Jews five times received I forty stripes save one —thrice was I scourged, once was I stoned, thrice I suffered shipwreck, a night and a day I have been in the deep, in journeyings often, in perils of rivers, in perils of robbers, in perils from my own countrymen, in perils from the Gentiles, in perils from the city, in perils in the wilderness, in perils in the sea, in labour and travail, in watchings often, in hunger and thirst, in fastings and cold and nakedness. Besides these things, that which cometh on me daily, the care of all the churches. The God and Father of the Lord Jesus Christ who is blessed for evermore knoweth that I lie not.

In what have I done you wrong ? Is it a crime that I proclaimed to you the glad tidings of God without fee or reward ? You insinuate about money. Even when I was in want did I ever let one of you contribute to my support ? Why ? Because I love you not ? God knoweth that I love you. But what I do I will continue to do that I may cut off ground of slander. For these men whom you follow are false and deceitful, clothing themselves in the garb of Apostles of Christ. No wonder. Even Satan their master can transform himself into an angel of light.

I do not think those Jerusalem visitors were very happy as this letter was read out next Sunday in Church. I am afraid I rather enjoy seeing them get what they deserve.   But Paul did not enjoy it.   He is too big a man to enjoy scolding.   And his letter closes on a kindly note.

I warn you all.   But I trust I shall not have need of severity. Finally, brethren, farewell. Reform what is amiss. Be of one mind.   Live in peace and the God of love and peace shall be with you.   The grace of Our Lord Jesus Christ and the love of God and the fellowship of the Holy Ghost be with you all.

CHAPTER XIII

FAITH AND WORKS

TITUS was sent back to Corinth with this Second Epistle, and soon after Paul followed it in person. He came to Corinth to encourage the faithful, to punish the wrongdoers, to excommunicate those who were wilfully obstinate in their sin. And so, in some degree, he brought peace to that distracted Church.

But scarce had he accomplished this, when, while he still remained in Corinth—like a bolt from the blue came tidings from Galatia of the very same trouble and worse, because the fickle Galatians were more easily led away. Again the Church was in serious danger, and Paul had to buckle on his armour and again spring into the breach. Hence comes the Epistle to the Galatians, and a few weeks later, while his heart is full of the subject, he wrote his majestic Epistle to the Romans, for which the Galatian Epistle provided the rough draft.

It is manifestly impossible in my limited space to comment on these great Epistles. But it is most important for your understanding of the Epistles that you should see clearly what Paul was fighting for ever since that day when he brought it before the Council of Jerusalem, and that you should realise that, humanly speaking, during that fight the very existence of the Christian Church was trembling in the balance. If Paul was beaten, Christianity might have survived as an Eastern sect, as a hanger-on of Judaism, but the great, universal, world-wide Catholic Church for all humanity would never have been.

II

Let us state the question in dispute. Here are the two sides :

(1) Salvation by the Works of the Law.

(2) Salvation by Surrender to and Faith in the Son of God.

What is meant by the works of the Law ?

Originally, in purer days, it meant real devotion to God, fenced in by concrete rules, such as the Ten Commandments, to guide the people. This is what the Law meant originally. This is what the Prophets fought to win back.

But Jewish religion had sadly deteriorated. The few rules of guidance grew and grew as priests and rabbis and scribes went on " fencing the Law " for centuries, till these external rules numbered hundreds, many of them petty and tedious and vexatious, and as they grew the soul died out of them and the external rules became substitutes for the living God. If you do these things you have won your salvation. If you fail you are lost. And so God became a great taskmaster, whose rules were hard to count and hard to know and harder to do. The common crowd who did not know them were damned. " This people who knoweth not the Law are cursed,"* said the Pharisees. They cannot be saved. The earnest, conscientious Jew who tried to keep them fully had a very bad time. You remember how Paul tells in the Epistle to the Romans, his own miserable experience of trying to win salvation by the Law. "I cannot succeed. I try hard. I often fail. And if I succeed in one hundred points, and fail in one point, I am guilty of all." It was a miserable, distressing struggle.

You remember the stern indignation of Jesus about the burden of these rules, and how He castigated the teachers till, in their rage, they arose and crucified Him. " Woe unto you Scribes and Pharisees, hypocrites. Ye shut the Kingdom of Heaven on men by your rules. Ye bind grievous burdens on their shoulders. Woe unto you, ye blind guides. Ye cleanse the outside of the cup and platter (by your external rules), while within it is full of evil and excess. Ye give tithes of such trifles as mint and anise and cummin and leave undone the weightier matters of the Law, judgment and mercy and faith. Ye fools and blind ! Ye whited sepulchres ! Away with your petty little commandments of the Law ! There are only two real commandments of the Law. Thou shalt love the Lord thy God with all thy heart and Thou shalt love thy neighbour as thyself. On these two hang all the Law and the Prophets."

Now you see what Paul was fighting for, what the Prophets were fighting for, what Jesus was fighting for. You see what is meant by the works of the Law, with which Jerusalem Christians wanted to fetter the gospel. An ecclesiastical code of troublesome,

* John vii. : 49.

complicated, external rules with the soul gone out of them. And Jewish rules, too. Note this especially. For if the gospel was to be put in these Jewish fetters— if Jewish rules were to be made burdens on the Greek and Roman and Celt and Saxon, what likelihood was there of a great world-wide Church of Christ ?

Do you wonder that Paul fought fiercely, indignantly ? Do you wonder that he felt heartbroken when the tidings came that the Galatians had been drawn away from the freedom of his gospel ? Can you wonder that this Epistle to the Galatians is a very war cry ?

III

Let us look at this Galatian Epistle.

It begins abruptly—severely. It is the only Epistle beginning without words of praise and thankfulness. He is greatly hurt that those whom he loved should take sides with his enemies. He contradicts the falsehoods and calumnies. He tells the story of his life and his call by Christ. But chiefly he insists that this doctrine of the Judaisers would destroy the very essence of Christianity and reduce it from an inward spiritual life to a dry, external ceremonial system.

He meets their objections, " Then what use is the Law ? " The Law, he says, was very useful as originally given, as a check on humanity in the preparation stage for Christ. Child rules are necessary for children. But we are past that child stage now that Christ has come. The Law, too, is as a tutor, a child-leader to bring us to Christ. Finding that we cannot of ourselves keep God's laws, we want the loving Christ and the power of the Holy Ghost. If you will read the Epistle over rapidly all at one sitting, again and again, keeping Paul's purpose in mind, you will easily get into the attitude of the writer, and see what an interesting and valuable letter it is.

IV

Now comes his greatest literary work, the Epistle to the Romans. He had long looked forward to visiting the great metropolis of the world. There was no church yet in Rome founded by any Apostle. It was probably at this time just a gathering of Christians from many parts, gravitating to the great city. We have not space here to discuss the origin of the Roman Church. At any rate, Rome was the metropolis of the Empire, the centre of influence, and Paul felt the importance of giving to the Christians there a full and clearly reasoned statement of the Gospel. Perhaps he felt, as old age was creeping on him, that it was full time he should lay down, in a systematic treatise, the great thoughts that had grown in him by God's inspiration through all his chequered life.

Therefore, this is not a mere letter, called forth by some special need, as are other letters. This is a great theological treatise for the Church, bearing on the points of most importance at the time. And he gives special emphasis to the main question of the day—justification by faith in Christ as opposed to justification by the works of the Law. He had fought this battle fiercely in his Second Epistle to the Corinthians. He had fought it at white heat in the

stress of the conflict in the Epistle to the Galatians.
Now he writes more calmly. For the victory is almost
won. The catholic position of the Church is fairly
well assured against the assault that might have
destroyed it.

V

I have no thought of commenting on this noblest
and deepest of all Paul's pronouncements. It is far
too long a subject to deal with in detail here. But
avoiding its deeper depths, let me try to give
some little idea of its main thought to help you in
reading it.

After saluting them, and introducing himself, he
tells why he is writing, and why he intends to come
to them. " As the Apostle to the Gentiles I owe to
them, I am debtor to them to bring the good tidings.
I am debtor to Greek and Barbarian. So as much as
in me is, I am ready to preach the Gospel to you at
Rome also.

First realise this. You know in your hearts that
you need a Saviour, because all, Jews and Gentiles,
have broken God's law. You may say the Gentiles
never had that law to break. Yes, they have. The
Law of God in their conscience. So all have sinned.
And we can do nothing ourselves to save ourselves.
We are all shut up under condemnation.

Now comes God's good news. The loving Father
has provided the remedy, a free gift through Christ.
On His side it is free, generous giving ; on our side
it is free unmeritorious receiving. No room for
bargaining, or independence, or pride. It is God's

free gift to men undeserving. You cannot save your-selves. " Through the works of the Law can no flesh living be justified."

God makes no distinction. Jew or Gentile, great sinner or small, all are welcome to Him. To every penitent soul He will give not only forgiveness for the past, but the power of the Holy Ghost for their future. Notice how emphatically he dwells on this power of the Holy Ghost. To win this while we were yet sinners Christ died for us. Nothing can keep back His love for the penitent. " Neither death nor life, nor angels, nor principalities, nor powers are able to separate us from the love of Christ."

Then comes the chapters on the deep mysteries of God's calling and election, so frequently misunder-stood. Here he gives the mysterious hope to poor Israel, who has lost its high calling for the present. One day all Israel shall be saved.

So he closes, Pray for me that I may come to you in the fulness of the gospel, and may the God of peace be with you all. Amen.

CHAPTER XIV

The Works of the Law in the Twentieth Century

THIS is a postscript to the preceding chapter. I have been thinking myself into the place of the reader of that chapter as he follows St. Paul in his strenuous fight against the Jewish Christians as to the meaning of Christ's religion. He can see distinctly the two sides in the controversy, the Religion of Faith in Christ *versus* the Religion of the Works of the Law, or in other words, the Devotion of the Heart to God *versus* the Keeping of External Rules.

Is he thinking that though all this may be interesting as a controversy of men of the first century, yet it has little practical bearing on men of the twentieth century, who have quite passed beyond such thoughts ? I think he is, and my purpose here is to point out that he is wrong. The Religion of the Works of the Law as opposed to the Religion of Devotion to God belongs to the twentieth century as much as to the first. It belongs to all ages. It belongs deep down in the bedrock of human nature.

II

Let us go over the two sides again. First look at Paul's side.

This, said Paul, is the Glad Tidings revealed by Christ. God is not the Great Taskmaster, coldly watching to see if you keep or break external rules. God is the loving Father, who cares tenderly for all His poor children, and cannot bear to lose one of them. He seeks not the cold keeping of external rules, but the warm affection and devotion of His child. His supreme purpose is the making of beautiful, lovable character. That is what He wants for His child That is Salvation. That is Heaven.

It is not a case of your anxious independent effort to win Salvation by your own deservings. Conscience tells you you cannot. Every earnest man who ever tried it knows his failure. God cares more than you care. So the Eternal Son of God has taken hold for you. He died to win forgiveness for you. His Holy Spirit is inspiring in you noble thoughts and strengthening you to noble deeds. Trust yourself to Christ. He makes Himself responsible for you. Let yourself go. Trust yourself utterly to His loving care for you here and hereafter. And His love for you will win yours in return.

III

Beside this put the Religion of the Works of the Law as St. Paul knew it. It means not only the earning of Salvation by one's own independent efforts, but the earning of it by ceremonial observances, and the keeping of certain external rules. This appeals not only to the pride, but also to the indolence and

unspiritualness of human nature.   The whole teaching
of the Prophets is a continuous protest against it.
The relation of the heart to God, they insist, is what
supremely matters.   A well-known passage of Micah
gives concisely the attitude of all his brethren.

> Wherewith shall I come before the Lord and bow myself
> before the High God ?   Shall I come before Him with burnt
> offerings and calves of a year old ?   Shall I give my firstborn
> for my transgressions, the fruit of my body, for the sin of my
> soul ?
> He hath shewed thee, O man, what is good.   What doth
> the Lord require of thee but to do justly and love mercy and
> walk humbly with thy God ?*

But the prophets had been long dead, and in the
centuries between, religion had drifted back to the
old low standpoint.   Now again, in the hands of Scribes
and Pharisees, it had come to mean the winning of
God's favour by keeping external rules.

This was the Religion of the Works of the Law
in the days of Paul.   " Here are certain external rules,
moral and ceremonial.   He that doeth these things
shall live by them.   You need not do more.   You must
not do less.   If you succeed, then, by your own efforts
and deservings, you have won.   If not, you have
failed."

Even in the light of old prophetic teaching this
attitude would be wrong.   How much more so after
Christ had revealed the tenderness of God's fatherhood.   Apart from its hopelessness, it was such a
cold, unloving attitude towards the Father.   It was
a cold, independent legal claim upon God.   Like as
if your boy should coldly say, So long as I behave

F   * Micah vi.

decently, and learn my lessons, my father is bound to support me, and leave me his money when he dies —when you know how you lie awake at night thinking and planning for him, and that all the joy of life would go if your boy went wrong.

IV

Now let us see how this Religion of the Works of the Law worked out in practice.

The nobler type of Pharisee, like Saul of Tarsus, before his conversion, set himself diligently, with minute scrupulosity to keep the two hundred and forty-eight precepts, and the three hundred and forty-six prohibitions. But it did not satisfy his soul. In his higher moments he felt the unreality and hollowness of mere external rules, and doubted if he could ever really win God's full approval. " I have kept certain precepts. I have failed in others, and he that offendeth in one point is guilty of all." Paul himself tells of this miserable time in his own life. All the same you cannot help respecting men like him who tried to do hard things.

But—and this is what I want especially to emphasise here—the average Jew did not bother about all these fine-drawn rules. In fact, he did not know them all. He kept the same attitude of winning salvation by his deeds. But he had an easy conscience. He chose the few prominent rules that appealed to him, and left out the rest. He must be circumcised, and go to the Festivals, and not be an idolator, or a thief, or an adulterer. He was quite conscientious about living up to this easy standard.

But he was satisfied with himself when he had done so. His conscience took him no further. The devotion of his heart to God did not come in. So long as he kept his little external code, he did not see what further claim God had on him. He resented any further claim. No higher light from above was allowed to come in to rouse him to nobler things.

This was the lower view, the average man's view of the Religion of the Works of the Law.

V

Now I repeat my assertion that this Religion of the Works of the Law is as common in our day as in that of St. Paul. And the worst of it is—pay special attention to this—that is not the nobler type of it, as in the earnest Pharisee scrupulously struggling to keep all the precepts, but the lower type, the religion of the average Jew. Like the average man in that day, the average man in our day leaves out the relation of his heart to God. To satisfy his conscience he picks out a little modicum of rules as they fit himself, and as they are sanctioned by the public opinion of his class. He makes his religion the keeping of these few easy external rules, without ever a thought of the father's real claim upon his child. " My son, give me thine heart."

" Without ever a thought," I said. No, that is not quite true. Now and then the thought obtrudes, that what he has learned about God's love and Christ's atonement on the Cross ought to make some claim on his heart. But since he is not prepared for surrender to that claim, he avoids thinking about it.

" I am not a very religious man, he says, but I'm not a bad sort of fellow. I am not doing anything wrong, and I don't think God has anything much against me."

VI

Now I want to locate this twentieth century man or woman. You must have noticed that, whether there be any heart relation to God or not, all decent people in a Christian country have a certain little standard of life, rather a low, easy standard, but about which they are most conscientious. Not a bad little standard so far as it goes, and so long as they do not mistake it for religion. Religion must have God in it. Religion means, in its essence, the relation of the heart to God.

The average decent schoolboy has three main laws. He must not lie, nor bully a little chap, and above all things, he must not be a sneak, to tell tales on another fellow.

The average soldier feels that he must not disgrace his uniform, must be loyal to his country at any cost, must be brave even unto death where duty calls him. And he is doing very fine things to-day on these few rules.

The average decent woman has her minimum standard. She must be chaste, must care for her husband and children, must send her children to church, even if she does not go herself.

The average business man's conscience insists that he must be honest, must live a decent life, must care for his wife and children, and if he can afford it, must give something to charity or to patriotic funds.

Even the selfish, idle rich has his little works of the Law. He must be polite, he must live respectably, he must obey the code of honour in his set, he must rigidly, at any cost, pay his gambling debts—debts of honour he calls them—even if he be careless about other debts.

Each is most conscientious about this little standard of his, and quite pleased with himself when he keeps up to it. Of course, he adds a little more to these foundation laws. But if he be the man that I am thinking of, he never thinks of adding the supreme thing, God. His heart is in no personal relation to God. There is no love to God, no gratitude to God, no sense of duty to God, no dissatisfaction with his life, no deep penitence, no passionate prayer, no longing that God's Holy Spirit should lead him to anything higher than this.

His conscience is strict about these three or four life laws. So far it is good. But his conscience is quite content with that little standard. He shuts out all the light that would lead him to a higher standard. He is nervously afraid of the very idea of aiming at the highest and surrendering his life to the guidance of God wherever it might lead. No. He feels satisfied with himself at present by keeping his standard low. He might be very much dissatisfied with himself if he let God raise his standard. And he does not want to be dissatisfied. He feels all right— God, he thinks, has nothing to complain of.

This is the modern man's " Justification by the Works of the Law," without thinking of the relation of his heart to God. He is, in short, the Pharisee, but he is much lower than the Pharisee. For he has made himself a low standard. The Pharisee at least had a difficult standard. " I fast twice in the week. I give tithes of all that I possess." He has a much easier rule.

God wants to lift him up to be the noblest thing in the Universe. But he prefers to live down with his low little standard.

I am thinking of some such men that I have met at a time when one aims at heart-to-heart talks— when the man perhaps is dying, and one wants to try and diagnose his spiritual condition. Here is a frequent answer : " Well, I don't think God has anything against me. I have never cheated in business, nor wilfully injured another. I am not an extortioner, nor unjust, nor an adulterer, nor even as this publican. I fast twice—no, I don't do that. I give tithes of— no, I do not. But anyway, I respect religion. I'm not an unbeliever. I go to Church sometimes, if it is not raining, or if I'm not tired. I am quite conscientious about this."

But if one asks him, " What of the relation of your heart to God ? Have you any love to the Father in Heaven. Any gratitude to the blessed Lord ? Would it make much difference to you if the story of the Gospel were proved false ? Are you very dissatisfied and penitent ? Are you praying that God would lift you up to be a noble servant of Christ to your life's end ! " He smiles at it. " That is all high-falutin sort of parson's talk. I think I am doing very well."

Here is the easy modern edition of the religion of the deeds of the Law. It is an easy religion. Like the children's lesson books, " French without tears," " Latin without tears," this is Religion without tears. It does not cost much, and it does not accomplish much. It makes a man satisfied and independent of Christ. But oh, it shuts out the light from Heaven, and keeps him from the beautiful progressive growth of soul which God designs for him. The man is shutting out the Christ out of his life, and his soul is growing flabby and withered and rotten within him.

VIII

Let no one misunderstand or misrepresent this teaching. I read an infidel book lately, which represents the Gospel as teaching that doing right was less important than believing something about Christ—that trying to do good works might land you in hell. Intelligent Christians do not talk like that. The Bible says it was for good works God created us. " God created us unto good works "—" shew me thy faith by thy works "—" be careful to maintain good works," etc.

The contrast I present to you is not between right conduct and right belief—but between the man who, apart from any heart relation to God, makes his own few self-chosen external rules, and considers that obedience to them justifies him with God, and is quite satisfied with himself—between him, I say, and the man who, feeling his own sin, longing to rise to the highest finds out how God loves, finds out how Christ cares, and then casts himself on Him in humble trust, to be enabled to do such good works as he could never dream of by himself, and to go on to an eternity of such beautiful deeds for ever and ever.

And I say deliberately that any man living in the light of Christianity as we are—who is not penitently praying to get nearer to God, who is contentedly keeping his few rules of decent respectability and making them his cold legal claim on the Eternal Father— should have ringing in his ears the solemn warning of Scripture : " By the deeds of the Law shall no flesh living be justified. Except your righteousness exceed the righteousness of the Scribes and Pharisees ye shall in no case enter the Kingdom of Heaven."

That is Paul's attitude in his fight for religion.

PART IV

TO PRISON AND TO DEATH

PART IV

TO PRISON AND TO DEATH

CHAPTER XV

GOING UP TO JERUSALEM

IT is the month of February, A.D. 58. Paul has
been nine months in Europe. He has accomplished
great things in that time. He has laid the foundations of the Catholic Church of the West.

One would think he might rest now. He has had
a hard life. He has done a great work. He is growing
old. The time of youthful enthusiasm ought to be
over for him. But some men never grow old at heart.
To Paul all that he has accomplished seems only a
beginning. He is dreaming of far greater doings in
the future.

His vision is expanding to the far horizon—to the
limits of the Roman Empire, to the shores of Spain,
to the Pillars of Hercules, where the world ends. Even
there he means to carry the banner of the Cross
committed to him by Jesus on the Damascus road.
And the centre of his vision is the Imperial City, Rome.

We have hints of his great project in the epistle
which he has just sent to Rome.

" I have long wished to see you. I hope soon to come to you on my way to Spain. I must first go to Jerusalem to meet the chiefs of the Church, and to bring my collections for the poor. When that is done I hope to start for Rome. If it be God's will. But pray for me earnestly that I may be delivered from the dangers before me in Judea, that I may come with joy to you, that through the will of God I together with you may find rest."

Yes ! Paul, through the will of God you will come to them in Rome, but in a way that you little dream of to-day. And through the will of God you will find rest in Rome—the rest that will come to yor through the headsman's axe !

II

Now in this month of February, 58, he is starting from Corinth on the beginning of that expedition. But first he must go to Jerusalem to meet the heads of the Church, and to bring the moneys collected for the poor. Young Timothy is with him, and Luke and Trophimus the Ephesian, and four other delegates from the churches of Asia, probably bringing with them the moneys collected in their towns.

First to Jerusalem. He wants to get there in time for the Passover. It is not easy to get a passage just now, for all over the land the caravans are on the march, the Passover pilgrims are assembling. Down at the harbour he finds quite a crowd of them already waiting for a ship.

And soon he finds that it is an ugly crowd, and dangerous. Black looks and muttered curses greet him as he comes. There is no time when a fanatic crowd is so excited and inflamed as just before a religious festival, and if Paul had been a wiser man he would have chosen some other port than that of Corinth, where he was so well known and so well hated by the Jews. They are already pointing him out, the renegade who speaks blasphemous words against Moses and the Law. They are biding their time. A crowded ship on a dark night is a capital place to knife a man or hustle him overboard. Paul's friends get wind of the treacherous plot, so they have to decide to start overland through Macedonia.

It is an ominous beginning for the great expedition to the ends of the earth. And there is no chance now of being in Jerusalem for the Passover. However, it is a pleasant journey with pleasant friends, in the beautiful spring-time just before Whitsuntide, and it takes them through towns where dear old friends will meet them. I think Paul got sick with his chronic disease when they came to Philippi, for I find that he and the physician Luke had to stay there while their party passed on to Troas. If so, it was not a bad place to fall sick, amid the best beloved of his converts, Lydia and the jailer, and all the rest of them.

Which suggests to us not to think gloomily of Paul's life in spite of its dangers and troubles. Such friendships around him everywhere made a large compensation. I wish we had more time for such friendships in this hurried life of ours. There are many pleasant friendships in the careless world, but it is no cant to say that Christian men's friendships grow closer in the common tie of friendship with their Lord, and the hope in common that their friendships shall be eternal in the boundless life of the Hereafter. True friendships are what give colour to life. Someone once asked Charles Kingsley what he was most thankful for in his life. " That God gave me friends," he said.

So with Paul. He had no wife or child or family ties. But God gave him friends. If few men had more bitter enemies than he, few men also had more devoted friends. And that meant happiness in spite of all his troubles.

III

He spent Passover week in Philippi. Passover fell that year on Thursday, April 7th, and the Christian Jews were keeping the festival. But no longer as a mere Jewish celebration. Already Paul had put into it the Christian meaning, " Christ our Passover is sacrificed for us, therefore let us keep the feast." It was the beginning of our present day celebration of Good Friday and Easter.

Next day he and Luke left Philippi and five days later caught up their friends at Troas, that classic ground by the plains of Troy from which he had started last year on this European trip. Here they had all to wait for a ship till Monday, the 18th. This gave them a Sunday in Troas, and Luke has jotted down in his diary an interesting picture of their Church service in the upper room. You feel that the picture is by an eyewitness. You see the picture before him, the eager assembly, the many lights, the windows flung open in the warm night. You see him uneasily watching the lad Eutychus in the upper window dozing and dropping asleep, and as the sermon goes on borne down by deep sleep till, with a startled cry, before anyone can reach him, he falls out through the open window three stories high. An upper window ledge is not a good place for sleeping in sermon time.

There is not much sleep for anyone else that night, for the ship sails at dawn. After their Communion service together, Paul sees his comrades on board and starts off alone on a twenty-mile walk to catch them up at the next port. He wants a long walk. He wants a rest from people for the present. He wants to be alone for quiet thought and communion with God. There is much to think about. The events of the last few weeks have shaken his confidence. Forebodings are in his heart that his great expedition to Spain is falling through. Somehow he feels that the brightest days of his ministry are probably over, and that the future holds hard times for him. Down the cemetery road, past the hot springs of Troas, through the oak woods, he wends his way, deep in thought all day, and at night catches up the ship at Assos.

IV

On an evening ten days later we pick up his party again as they enter the harbour at Miletus. The ship had passed Ephesus without stopping, but there was time at Miletus to send a messenger to summon at least the presbyters of Ephesus to meet him. Next day they arrive at Miletus, and here we get another of the graphic pictures in Luke's diary.

There is the ship unloading her cargo, the sailors shouting and singing at their work. Out on the sands a sad little group of clergy gathered to say good-bye to their master and friend. Paul is speaking :—

" I leave Ephesus in your charge. Take heed to yourselves," he says, " and to the flock over which the Holy Ghost hath made you overseers, to feed the church of God which He hath purchased by His own blood. Give to them of your best. Remember the words of the Lord Jesus how He said, ' It is more blessed to give than to receive.' Ye know how I bore myself among you since the first day that I set foot in Asia, teaching publicly and from house to house repentance towards God and faith towards Our Lord Jesus Christ. Now I am going away from you, not knowing what is before me, saving that in every place the Holy Spirit testifies that bonds and afflictions await me. What matter provided I finish my course faithfully and the ministry which I received of the Lord Jesus. So I have to say good-bye to you, a long good-bye, for ye among whom I lived proclaiming the glad news shall see my face again no more. Be watchful. Be faithful. Farewell to you all. I commend you to God and to the word of His grace who is able to build you up and give you an inheritance among them that are sanctified. Now let us kneel down and pray to Him to have you in His holy keeping."

And they all kneel down sobbing through the prayer, " sorrowing most of all for the word which he had said that they shall see his face again no more."

So they parted, " tearing themselves away," and again we realise how men held him in their hearts, and how deeply he meant those affectionate greetings in his letters to the churches when he was far away from them.

V

Another week of delightful sailing in those sunny April days past Coos and Rhodes on its island of roses, on to Patara where they change ship for Palestine. The third day he can see from the deck the highlands of Cyprus open up before him—Cyprus the home of his old friend Barnabas, now with his Lord in the spirit land. " Ah, Barnabas, I wish I had been less im- patient with you that day at Antioch ! "

They spent a week in Tyre, famous in Jewish pro- phecy. There the brethren warned him of the danger in Jerusalem, and there was repeated the scene at Miletus, " they all with their wives and children accompanied us out of the city, and kneeling down on the beach we prayed together and said good-bye."

VI

Now they are in beautiful Cæsarea, the capital and seat of government—only three days from Jerusalem. There are fourteen days to spare before Pentecost, and it is pleasanter to spend them here with friends than in Jerusalem, where his reception is more doubt- ful. Paul is the guest of Philip the evangelist, a man after his own heart, with his own broad views. We remember when Philip was ordained one of the Seven Deacons—when he dared to preach the Gospel to the heretic Samaritans—when he baptised the black eunuch of Candace, queen of the Ethiopians, and leaving him, preached from town to town till he came to Cæsarea. That was twenty years ago, and here he is in Cæsarea still with his four daughters, the virgins that did prophesy.

What memories he would bring back to Paul as they sit together in the evenings talking over old times —that day when they had been present at the stoning of Stephen, the time when Paul had chased him and his comrades from Jerusalem, and how their loving Lord from the heavens had overruled all for good, how Paul's pursuit of the disciples had spread the Gospel more widely, how Philip, far away from the narrowing influences of Jerusalem, was more in touch with Paul's wide views than were the Christians at headquarters.

And as they talked, young Luke was surely listening and making voluminous notes for his book. It was good for Paul to get these restful days in Cæsarea, the last he should have of such restful days for many a year to come. Even these were broken by warnings of coming dangers, and friends weeping and beseeching him not to go on. But Paul's purpose was fixed. He saw where duty lay. Like his Master before him amid similar warnings, " he steadfastly set his face to go to Jerusalem."

CHAPTER XVI

RIOT AND ARREST

ANOTHER week has passed. Paul is in Jerusalem. The last visit of his life to the Holy City. And the saddest. He had come with boyish eagerness in the old college days long ago. He had come back, a man shaken by many emotions after his vision on the Damascus road. He had come up with Barnabas to win his battle for the freedom of the Church. Now he is come for the last time with foreboding in his heart "ready not only to be bound, but, if necessary, to die at Jerusalem for the name of the Lord Jesus."

He is staying with Mnason of Cyprus, an "old disciple" who has a house in Jerusalem. Through his window he can see the Pentecost crowds in the street, the crowds that he had been accustomed to since early days. "Parthians and Medes and Elamites, and dwellers in Mesopotamia, in Pontus and Asia." And Asia! He does not like the look of that crowd from Asia. There is a group of them passing now, easily recognised in their bright national costume so familiar to him in his three years at Ephesus. He could very well do without these, his bitterest opponents, the bigots who hated him and stirred up riots against him everywhere he went. He knows very well that they will be his chief danger in Jerusalem. The less he sees of them the better.

II

But he cannot avoid them. For the brethren at Jerusalem have put him in an embarrassing position. On the whole, one feels disappointed at their attitude. Just a week ago he had entered the city. They do not seem to have provided hospitality for him, the greatest churchman of them all. He had a pleasant welcome from friends on his arrival. But the next day was a serious ordeal when he appeared before the assembled church. Some of them were in full agreement with him, but he knew that many were quite out of sympathy with his broad views about the Gentiles. They could not agree that the despised heathen should be received into the Church on a level with the ancient people of God. So Paul was not at all received with the unanimous enthusiasm that we should have expected.

He had brought them a large money collection for the poor, which had taken years of thought and execution. He gave them a glowing account of his work for the Lord—of all the heathen converted to Christ, all the important churches that he had founded in the West. But I think Luke, his biographer, is disappointed at their response, judging from the entry in his diary.

True, "they glorified God." They could hardly help doing that. Then immediately they chilled him with the cautious advice : " Brother, you must be careful. Our people here are very much concerned about your teaching. You not only abolish all distinction between the Gentiles and the chosen people ; you seem even to go farther. You speak very

unguardedly.   They think you are overthrowing Moses
and the Law.   Now be advised by us.   Be very
cautious.   Clear yourself of suspicion.   Do not get
religion into discredit.   Shew yourself publicly a good
Jew.   Here are four poor men who have a Jewish
vow.   Take charge of them publicly.   Be their sponsor
and go to the Temple with them daily, paying their
charges for shaving their heads and other purification
ceremonies.   So shall men see that you are loyal to
the Jewish rules."

III

No doubt it was wise advice, if only it had come
at some other time, not just then when his pulses were
throbbing with the excitement of his great story of the
triumph of Christ amongst the heathen.   If you want
a favourable hearing for your doctrine you must not
antagonise people unnecessarily.   The Church was
in a critical position at this transition time from
Judaism to Christianity.   If the church at Jerusalem
at this crisis had repudiated Paul the results might
have been disastrous.   The Church always needs not
only eager enthusiasts, but also farsighted prudent
men, and it was God's good providence that a wise,
cautious man like James should be at the helm just
then.

Still, it is possible to overdo caution ; and it is
possible to put it at the wrong time.   One can imagine
the disappointment of Paul, after his passionate speech
about the glory of Christ and the conversion of countless heathen, that their prominent thought should be
the soothing of popular prejudice by conformity in

what to him were but the "weak and beggarly elements." As if the Church of England thirty years ago should meet a famous missionary who had come back in triumphant enthusiasm to tell of a continent won for Christ, "Brother, we want you to be in church to-morrow, that the people may see you wear the black gown in the pulpit, or that they may see you taking the Eastward Position at the altar."

Of course Paul could conscientiously do it. It was quite right for him as a Jew, and it might conciliate Jewish Christians even though it might also be misunderstood by Gentile converts. What seems to have been forgotten was that it would put him in undesirable prominence amongst the excited fanatic Jews from every land who were daily crowding the temple courts. Especially those Jews from Asia who had been pursuing him with slanders and murderous plots all through his ministry.

IV

On the seventh day they got him—those Jews from Asia. That morning they had suddenly recognised him in the streets, walking with his Gentile friend, Trophimus the Ephesian, and now they see him in the temple with his four poor men, and they are but too ready to suspect that he had brought in the Gentile into the holy place. He had not done anything of the kind, but suspicious people will believe anything. Straightway the fierce hatred is flashing in their eyes, and with a wild shout of rage, the men of Asia are upon him. "Men of Israel, help! This is the wretch that teaches everywhere against Moses and the Law and the Temple of God. Now he has brought Gentiles into the temple, and polluted the holy place!"

The defilement of the temple was the unspeakable crime. Even the Roman authorities had to be most careful about that. In a moment the rumours had spread among the fanatic crowd, and in another moment they have rushed him. He is struck to the ground, and flung violently down the steps through the Beautiful Gate. And straightway the gates are shut behind him, lest the Temple should be desecrated by murder. The murder does not matter so much, provided it is done outside. Ah, Paul, it will go hard with you now unless the Christ of the Damascus road be watching you! There is no mercy in that trampling mob now that they have got you down.

But his time has not yet come. The Roman police are well trained in riots, and before he well has time to commend his soul to God he hears the sharp military command, and the rush of armed men, who lifted him in their arms as they beat back the crowd. In spite of their quickness, he was nearly torn from them, and only that line of armed men, that line of bright, flashing steel on the stairs kept them from following into the barracks.

Behind that line of steel, the chief Captain, Claudias Lysias, looks at his prisoner, all bruised and bleeding, but calm and undaunted, as he faces the crowd. Paul had been close to death too often to be much disconcerted. Calm and undaunted, he turns to the chief captain.

"May I speak unto thee, Captain?"

" What ? Can you speak Greek ? I thought you were that rascal Egyptian who led the Passover riots last year, whom we chased from the city with his band of assassins ! "

" No, I am a Jew, a citizen of Tarsus. I beseech thee for leave to speak to the people."

Surely an unexpected request from a man whom just now they had been trampling to death. But after all they were his own people, and he longed to help them. " Brethren, my heart's desire and prayer for Israel is that they should be saved."

Evidently, Claudius Lysias is impressed. A brave man is quick at recognising a brave man. He is curious, too, to see the result of this speech. Perhaps it might disperse the crowd for him without further bloodshed. But at any rate he will take no chances. He will keep that line of steel guarding the stairs.

V

Paul steps forward. His compelling personality and the sound of his words in their native tongue grips the crowd at once, and " immediately there is a great silence."

" Brethren, I am a Jew, like yourselves. Like you, I fiercely rejected the claim of Jesus to be the Messiah. Many of you remember how I hated His name and persecuted His followers as you do to-day. What changed me ? I will tell you." In simple, graphic words he tells the story of his life crisis, when the Christ of God appeared to him in glory on the Damascus road. " I am Jesus, whom thou persecutest ! " In that solemn hour He commissioned me from Heaven to proclaim the Righteous One whom I had seen and heard. " How could I resist him after that ? "

Up to this he holds his audience spellbound. It was a fascinating story, and quite new to most of them. But what more had Jesus said to him ? " He said to me, ' The Jews will not receive thy testimony about me,' He said, ' Depart, for I will send thee far hence unto the Gentiles ! ' "

Then in a moment pandemonium broke loose. The Gentile to be put in the place of the Jew ! They went wild with anger. " Down with the renegade ! Down with the traitor ! Away with such a fellow from the earth ! It is not fit that he should live ! "

And Claudius Lysias thought that it was just as well that he had kept that line of steel upon the stairs.

VI

But Claudius Lysias was vexed and disappointed. For Paul, instead of quieting the crowd, had roused them into raving lunatics. Of course, he could not understand Paul's speech. What had he said ? What was the trouble ? " Take him and strip him and examine him by scourging. We must get to the bottom of this, somehow."

Paul held his tongue as they bared his back and tied his hands for the torture. The rough Roman police would not understand him. But when an officer passed, he quietly asked, " Is it lawful for you to scourge a Roman citizen uncondemned ? "

" What ! A Roman citizen ! "

If there was one thing more than another promi-nent in the police regulations, it was the respect due to a man who could utter the proud boast, " Civis Romanus sum." Claudius Lysias is hurriedly called, and with new respect for his prisoner, and apprehension in his heart that he had maltreated a Roman citizen, he delivers Paul from the torture.

But he must try to understand the case. So next day he invites the Jewish Sanhedrin, and places Paul before him. Nothing comes of it. There is too much tension. Scarce had Paul begun his defence when the High Priest commanded to smite him on the mouth. Then very naturally Paul lost his temper. One only wonders that he kept it so long. " God shall smite thee, thou whited wall, who sittest there to judge me according to the law, and commandest me to be smitten contrary to the law ! "

He had not recognised that it was the High Priest, probably through his defective sight. But some of the judges must have enjoyed the thrust. The " whited wall " struck home in that company which knew the old hypocrite High Priest so well. Then, Paul, seeing that the council was composed of Pharisees and Sadducees, and that in the present temper of the assembly there was no chance of a fair hearing, cleverly divides his opponents, and plays them off against each other. " Men and brethren, I am a Pharisee and the son of a Pharisee, of the hope of a Resurrection I am called in question." Straightway the Pharisees swing around to his side in order to have a hit at their Sadducee opponents. The whole meeting is in uproar, and the chief captain has again to carry Paul off by force.

On the whole, Paul does not show up to his usual high level on this occasion. Critics have contrasted his attitude with the quiet, silent dignity of Jesus at his trial. It is not a fair criticism. It is expecting too much of the man. For Paul was not Jesus. And in the long, splendid record of that life to which the Spirit of God had raised him, one needs a reminder sometimes that he was only human like ourselves. That is the comfort of such biographies. If God's grace could so ennoble a poor, passionate human struggler, who was only a man like myself, may I not hope that He will also accomplish something worth while in me.

VII

I see Paul, that night, in his prison cell. His position is now very serious. Only the strong hand of the Roman police kept back the powerful faction that sought his life. And the Roman police must not interfere too much with that jealous people. They had got into trouble more than once for doing so. It was a bad time for Paul. Imprisonment and death face him. His enthusiastic scheme for carrying Christ's gospel to Rome and to the ends of the Empire seems frustrated. He has passed through two days of terrible strain, and he knows that the next day has more trouble in store. Most of us in his position would have gone to bed gloomily in that barrack cell. I dare say that Luke and Trophimus and Mnason, his host, had an anxious night thinking about him. I dare say Paul, too, felt despondent. It was only human. But I have no doubt that he took his despondency to the right place, and told God all about it, before he went to bed. So he could sleep quietly.

Many of us, I trust, have that habit, morning and evening, of spending some time with God upon the holy mount, telling Him of our plans and hopes and cares and anxieties and failings, and commending our lives to his loving care. We can understand why he slept quietly. As when the waves are tossing on the surface of the ocean the depths below are calm and untroubled, so when this man's outer life was harassed and disturbed, his inner life was hid with Christ in God. That is the secret of a Christian man's peace and " a stranger intermeddleth not with it." " If God be with us, who can be against us ? " If Christ approveth who is he that condemneth ?

And in his sleep in the visions of the night the Lord stood by him. If the Lord stood by him it did not greatly matter if men refused to do so. If we lived as close to Christ, perhaps we too should have such visions. " Cheer up, Paul ! Be of good cheer. You have borne witness faithfully for me in Jerusalem, you shall also bear witness for me in Rome."

Think what it meant to that desponding man. If all men were treating you with insult and contempt, and all life looked dark, what a pleasure if even a passing friend greeted you kindly. How it would bring tears to your eyes if some important person should clap you on the shoulder, " You are doing the right thing, my friend, I am heartily with you." But if it was the one whose approval was your highest ambition ; if it was the eternal Christ, your beloved Master and Friend ! And besides—" You shall also bear witness for me in Rome." Then, after all, perhaps his great expedition is not quite beyond hope.

At any rate, the Lord has said he should bear witness in Rome.

Never forget that inner secret of Paul's life, the constant realising of the close presence of his Lord. The whole value of this biography is lost if we forget Christ in thinking of His servant, if, in admiring his faith and courage and endurance, we lose sight for a moment of the secret of it all. He lived in Christ's presence. Behind, over the heads of priests and governors and howling mobs, he could always see Jesus. He sought only His approval. He knew Him for His friend in life or in death. In life he looked to Him for salvation and grace and comfort and help. " Not I, but the grace of God which was in me." In death he looked to Him for the joy of the Hereafter. " I desire to depart and be with Christ. I am persuaded that He is able to keep that which I have committed to Him against the Great Day."

Therefore his peace flowed like a river, the river whose streams make glad the city of God. God give us grace to live that life in some degree at least. For if we could but live thus close to our Lord we should not have a trouble in the world, but that we did not love Him enough and trust Him enough.

CHAPTER XVII

FOUR CÆSAREAN PICTURES

NEXT morning in the barracks Paul is seated in his cell, with a new, happy light in his eyes, as memory runs over that vision of the night, when suddenly he hears hurried footsteps in the corridor—his cell door is flung open, and his nephew, the son of his married sister in Jerusalem, rushes in all gasping and excited.

" What is the matter, my lad ? "

" Murder is the matter, Uncle Paul ! I have only just got ahead of the deputation who are coming up to interview the chief captain. They want him to bring you down again for the completing of yesterday's conference. But it is all a treacherous plot. If you leave these barracks you are a dead man. At a meeting last night more than forty of them have bound themselves under a curse not to eat or drink till they have killed you, and they are all lurking about the lanes near the barracks as I came in."

Evidently the lad was in a position to know. Which brings back our earlier conjectures about the attitude of Paul's family. I notice that in his visits to Jerusalem he never stays at his sister's house. I suggest that her husband was in the hostile camp—that he had been at that meeting last night and expressed his feeling against the plot when he got home. A man might object strongly to his brother-in-law without wishing to see him treacherously slain. And a woman, at such a time, would forget all her brother's faults and think only of the little Saul who played with her long ago in the old home in Tarsus. I think of her in the early morning stealing up to her son's bed and sending him post-haste off to the barracks.

II

Paul immediately sends the lad to the chief captain, and thus Claudius Lysias gets to know of the precious plot as he is preparing to meet those honourable gentlemen waiting in the anteroom. I wonder if the Roman officer kept his temper with them better than Paul had done yesterday.

The chief captain is a good deal worried over the matter. This prisoner of his is becoming an embarrassing responsibility. He is responsible for his safety as a Roman citizen. What with threatening mobs and scheming priests and fanatics, whose plots stop not short of assassination, he will be lucky if he can get him safe out of Jerusalem. Secretly he makes his plans. Under cover of the night we hear the tramp of horses and the soldiers assembling in the barrack square, nearly 500, so serious is the danger. All night the escort travels to the government headquarters at Cæsarea. You remember Paul had been staying in Cæsarea a week since with Philip the deacon. Philip and his daughters and the friends who had warned Paul of this danger last week see their prophecies fulfilled as their friend comes in bound, with a cavalry troop guarding him.

The governor is in his office and the officer of the guard hands him the chief captain's letter :—

Claudius Lysias unto his excellency Felix, sendeth greeting.

This man was seized by the Jews and was about to be slain by them when I rescued him, having heard that he was a Roman citizen. I found him accused of certain questions of their law, but of nothing worthy of death or of bonds. And discovering a dangerous plot against him I sent him to thee forthwith, charging his accusers to go down and speak before thee.

The Governor looks up from the letter :

" Of what province is this man ? "

" Cilicia, your excellency."

" I will hear the case when his accusers come. Meantime let him be kept in Herod's guardroom."

III

Thus began the Cæsarean imprisonment.

Two full years of the few that yet remained to him Paul was to waste in that prison in Cæsarea. It was a weary time. True, they were pretty good to him these Romans. They always were. There was something in the brave, quiet man that seemed to appeal to these rough pagan soldiers. ' Treat him kindly,' said Felix, ' and let his friends come and visit him.' So Philip and the friends in Cæsarea could come to see him, and Timothy and the travelling companions whom he had left in Jerusalem might sometimes come, and Luke had come down to stay near him and watch over his health.

I wonder what Paul did with himself during these two years. We hear of no epistles written as in his

later imprisonment. I can guess what Luke was doing.
I always think of Luke as going about with two manu-
script books in his baggage—one of them his diary
of his travels with Paul, some day to be completed
as the Acts of the Apostles—the other a book much
nearer completion, the notes for his coming gospel
dedicated to Theophilus.

There was not much material for the diary during
these two monotonous years, and, perhaps, for that
reason the few things that did happen get rather dis-
proportionate space and prominence. Perhaps, too,
he wanted to offset the Jewish opinion of his hero by
showing how favourably the unprejudiced outsiders
thought of him. He likes telling of the impression
made on Claudius Lysias and Felix and Festus and
King Agrippa and Julius the centurion.

St. Luke sketches for us in his diary four vivid little
pictures of these Cæsarean days. This is the first :

IV

It is the court room of the castle. Felix, the
governor, is on the judgment seat, and Ananias, the
high priest, is present among the accusers. He has
brought down a Jerusalem lawyer to conduct the
prosecution of the man who had called him a " whited
wall." The Pharisees and Sadducees have laid aside
their quarrel and are present in court combined
against the heretic.

Tertullus, the attorney, opens his case for the
prosecution by a fulsome eulogy of the judge. " The
Jews are specially fortunate in having so noble and
beloved a governor." (Of course, he knows that
Felix is the best hated governor they ever had. He

G

had bullied their people and killed their high priest. But you cannot say that in the pleadings.) " It is really a shame to trouble Your Excellency with this case. The Sanhedrin would have settled it themselves only that Claudius Lysias had, in a high-handed way, taken the man out of their hands. The man is a pestilent fellow, a disturber of the peace, a profaner of the temple and a ringleader of the sect of the Nazarenes, the followers of a fanatic, called Jesus, who was crucified by the late governor, Pontius Pilate, some years ago.

" That is our case, Your Excellency. The reverend gentlemen who are present will bear out what I have said."

But Felix knows too much about those reverend gentlemen. He wants to hear what Paul has to say. The poor prisoner arises with the chains on his hands and at once holds the attention of the court.

" I also am glad to have Your Excellency as judge, for from your long residence you are acquainted with Jewish affairs. I claim that the whole charge is false— all mere assertion. Where are the witnesses, the friends who knew me ; the men of Asia who seized me ? Why are they not here ? Where are the people who saw me bring Gentiles into the temple ? The truth is that twelve days ago I came up to Jerusalem to worship at Pentecost and to bring moneys collected for the poor. These people found me purified in the temple without crowd or tumult. They set on me and would have murdered me but for the interference of Claudius Lysias. I have done no wrong. I have nothing to confess but this, that after the way which they call heresy I worship the God of my fathers. I believe in the Messiah as looked for by the prophets, and look forward with hope in God to the resurrection of the dead."

There is something very convincing in the attitude of an honest man standing out amongst shams and hypocrites, and Felix, though no honest man himself, evidently felt it.   He knew very well what justice Paul would get if he were handed over to the Sanhedrin.

" The case is postponed," he said, " for further evidence.   Let the prisoner be put back, and treat him kindly—let him have all possible freedom, and let his friends come to visit him."

Evidently Paul had made a good impression on Felix.   So he went back to his prison.   And Luke, the beloved physician, came to attend him and to make more notes in that precious diary.

v

The next is a curious picture, strange and unexpected.

Paul is again before Felix.   Or rather, Felix is before Paul.   For Paul is now the dominant figure. This is no legal trial, but a private Court drawing-room called by Felix and his young bride, Drusilla, to hear the prisoner tell—of what think you ?   Of the faith of Jesus Christ for which he was in bonds ! What an extraordinary summons !   Surely Paul was as much surprised as we are.

I daresay it arose from mere idle curiosity—a bored little company of the Governor's guests seeking some distraction to pass a dull evening.   If there was anything more serious in it I do not believe it came from Felix at any rate.

One wonders if it was the young bride Drusilla. She is a Jewess and may wish to hear the teaching of her famous fellow-countryman. Probably she has heard already about Jesus Christ, for she is daughter of that King Herod who persecuted the Church and killed St. James, and in this very castle of Cæsarea five years ago was eaten of worms and died. Perhaps she is curious about this religion that seems to make that poor prisoner so happy. I doubt if she is very happy herself. She is young and gay and very beautiful, as were all the women of her family, but this does not always bring happiness. And her life does not tend to happiness. Her morals are no better than those of other Court ladies of the time. She is here to-day because this elderly profligate, Felix, a man of very unsavory reputation, has seduced her from her young husband and married her. So that neither she nor His Excellency are very respectable people from Paul's point of view.

But Paul says nothing rude to her. When Paul denounces people they are usually men. God only knows what is in that girl's heart or why she wanted to hear him speak of the faith of Jesus Christ. Paul does not judge her. But she hears him speak very plainly of the sins common in that Court. Probably she has heard of John the Baptist before Herod calling adultery by its right name, though the adulterer was a king, and losing his head for it. Here is another of the Baptist type. He has no thought of his own safety, only of his great message. He longs for her soul and all their souls. He feels himself, as he told the Corinthians, " an ambassador for Christ, beseeching men in Christ's stead, be ye reconciled to God, beseeching them that they receive not the grace of God in vain." I wish we clergy could always feel our positions as keenly. We should make men listen then.

Paul made them listen. We do not know what Drusilla felt, but as Paul reasoned of Righteousness and Temperance and the Judgment to come, Felix trembled. He had reason to tremble. Conscience had him by the throat. Many a scene of greed and treachery and lust and blood, of murdered men and dishonoured women, are there in his past life for memory to call up for that Judgment to come. For Felix's record in history is infamous, and conscience tells him bitter things as he listens to Paul.

But it is of no avail. Conscience is God's kind voice calling him to repentance. And for the moment it seems as if he wanted to repent. But like many another he does not want to repent just yet. " Go thy way, some other day at a more convenient season I will call thee again."

Ah ! some other day. We are all going to do great things some other day. Some other day we will repent and yield ourselves to Christ, and conquer our evil habits and be wonderfully good people. Every time a man says that he makes it less likely that he will do it. Every time you are brought in contact with Christ and higher things, and put off to " a more convenient season "—makes it less probable that that convenient season will ever come. Every such refusal draws blood, as it were, on the spiritual retina. Every such refusal hardens the heart. There is no ice so hard as that which melts a little on the surface and hardens again when the sunlight departs.

Ah Felix! that convenient season will never arrive for you. In a few months you will be cast out of your high position and vanish from history in obscurity and shame. That fair young wife will be swallowed up with her son in the terrible eruption of Mount Vesuvius. Well for you both if you had given heed to Paul that day when he reasoned of Righteousness and Continence and Judgment to come, and told you the meaning of the faith of Jesus Christ.

VI

The next scene is in the following year. The governor Felix is gone in disgrace to be tried in Rome on an accusation of the Jews, and to win favour with his accusers he meanly threw them a sop as he departed by leaving Paul bound. So after his two weary years, he is up again for trial before the new governor Festus. His enemies are more hopeful now. This governor is a new man. He does not know them as Felix did.

But Festus is not quite so simple as they think. For when they innocently suggest that Paul should be sent back to Jerusalem, where their assassins could easily reach him, " No," replies the governor, " Paul stays where he is. Bring your case before me here in Cæsarea."

So they are assembled again in the Great Hall of the Castle. But they are no better prepared than before. The same wrangling and abuse and accusations without proof, till Festus grew weary of the whole business, and wanted to get rid of it. " Here, Paul, what do you say to this suggestion that you go back to Jerusalem where people understand these perplexing subtleties ? Are you content to go back, and there be tried before me ? "

Paul knows too well what that would mean. He is sick of these delays. He sees little hope, since even the governor seems yielding now. Better risk everything to put an end to it. Instantly he throws out his challenge as a freeborn citizen of the Empire. " No, Your Excellency, I am not content, I stand here at Cæsar's judgment seat where I ought to be judged. I am willing to die if adjudged guilty of wrong, but I am not going back to Jerusalem to be murdered. I am a Roman citizen. I appeal unto Cæsar ! "

There was no evading that appeal. It was the proud privilege of every Roman citizen that he could always on just cause appeal to the Emperor. So after consulting his assessors, the governor pronounced the only possible sentence. " Hast thou appealed unto Cæsar ? Unto Cæsar then thou shalt go."

So the great case ended for the present, and the Jews had to go home baffled, outmanœuvred. And Paul wonderingly saw that in a far different way from what he had planned for himself, the word of the Lord was to be fulfilled. " Thou shalt one day go to bear witness for me in Rome "

VII

How little we can tell how our prayers will be answered. For years Paul had desired and prayed that he might go to Rome. Now in the Providence of God he is to go, but as a prisoner in chains. It seemed a most disappointing answer. But we know better now. One of the greatest treasures of Church and people for 2,000 years has been the noble group of epistles that Paul wrote from his prison in Rome, which we might never have had at all if he had gone as he desired, as a busy, active missionary.

It is a good thing to tell God all that we desire. Even if our prayers be foolish. God is not foolish. But it is a good thing, too, to leave the answer in His hands. Not to dictate the method of it or to say that if God does not answer as you expect you will cease to believe in prayer. For we are foolish children and don't know what is best.

I had a friend once who told me a curious thing. For years he had kept in a book a sort of Debit and Credit account with God. On the left-hand page the things he had most earnestly prayed for, and, opposite, the answers whenever they came. The result was very interesting. Sometimes the answers were opposite the prayers. Sometimes there was a blank where no answer came, and he often saw later that that too was good. And sometimes the answer came in a form quite different from what he expected.

I think that, too, would be Paul's experience. Years after this disappointing answer he writes to the Philippians from his Roman imprisonment : " I would have you to know that the things which have happened to me have fallen out rather unto the progress of the gospel."

Pray to God, but leave the issue in His hands, for God knows best and God cares.

The fourth picture in Luke's diary is a curious duplication of what happened in Felix's day. While waiting for his despatch to Rome there is again a sort of public drawing-room trial to amuse some distinguished guests of the governor, for King Agrippa, the son of Herod, with his wicked, profligate sister, Bernice, the Lucrezia Borgia of her day, had come down in state to visit the new governor in the palace where their young sister Drusilla had been mistress a few months ago. In course of conversation one day, Festus mentioned this prisoner of his who was accused by the Jews on some stupid question of religion, " and of one Jesus, who was dead, whom Paul affirmed to be alive."

King Agrippa had more connection with the matter than the governor knew—probably more than he knew himself. For Agrippa was a Jew, the last of the Herods, and the whole destinies of his house had been linked up with this Jesus whom Paul preached. His great grandfather Herod was the man who had slaughtered the Innocents at Bethlehem to destroy the child Jesus. His uncle Herod was the man who sent John the Baptist to death, and sent Jesus to Pilate with a scarlet robe of mockery on his shoulders. His father slew St. James and persecuted the Church. Agrippa had some reason to know about this religion of Paul.

" I would like to hear this man myself," he said.

" Well," replied the governor, " you shall hear him to-morrow."

" So on the morrow," I read, " when Agrippa was come, and Bernice with great pomp, and were entered into the place of hearing with the chief captains and principal men of the city at the command of Festus, Paul was brought in. . . . And Agrippa said unto Paul, ' Thou art permitted to speak for thyself.' And the prisoner arose with the chains on his hands before that brilliant assembly. He knew that nothing depended on this trial, since he had already appealed to Cæsar. But it was another opportunity to speak for his Lord.

" I think myself happy, King Agrippa, that I am to speak before a king who is my own countryman, and knows of the prophecies and hopes of our nation. I am accused of believing in that Messiah whom the prophets, for ages, have looked forward to. I know that He has come, and that God has raised Him from the dead whom Pilate crucified. You know the story, O King, better than His Excellency the Governor, who is but a stranger. Twenty years ago all Jerusalem was ringing with it, for these things were not done in a corner.

" Why should it be thought impossible with you that God should raise the dead ? I myself am no mere credulous enthusiast, I was more bitter than most men in my obstinate unbelief. I am known as the fiercest persecutor of the men who had been with Jesus, persecuting and slaying, and compelling them to blaspheme. Why do I believe ? Because I was forced to believe. Because that risen Messiah in His glory appeared to me and commissioned me in His name."

Then he repeats his oft-told story, how the Christ of God appeared to him on the Damascus road. " And He has sent me, O King, on a great mission to open men's eyes, to turn them from darkness to light, and from the power of Satan unto God, that they might receive remission of their sins by faith that is in Him. Wherefore, O king, I was not disobedient to the heavenly vision. That is the cause of this persecution, and of the Jews going about to kill me. But here I stand and must always stand, testifying both to small and great what the prophets and Moses did say that the Christ must suffer, and by the resurrection of the dead proclaim light to the people and to the Gentiles."

In the midst of this passionate appeal Festus interrupts. He is impatient of this foolish talk about a crucified Jew risen from the dead.

" Paul, you are beside yourself. Your great learning has made you mad."

" Nay, I am not mad, most noble Festus. The king will understand me. King Agrippa, you understand ? You believe the prophets ? I know that you believe them."

But Agrippa is not convinced, or is ashamed to respond. In good-natured banter he laughingly replies.

" With little persuasion,* Paul, you expect to make me a Christian ? "

But I can fancy the smile dying away as he hears the touching reply, in all sincerity, from that loving heart.

" I would to God that whether by much or by little

* We have to give up the familiar translation of the Authorised Version, the text of so many sermons, " Almost thou persuadest me to be a Christian." The Greek shows that this is no cry of a soul almost convinced, but the jest of a proud man who would scorn to believe. (See *Revised Version.*)

persuasion, not only thou, but all who hear me this day were such as I am except "—as he feels the chains rattle on his outstretched hand—" except these bonds."

No doubt those proud pagan lords would smile at such a wish, but would not any poor follower of Jesus to-day understand it ? Paul knew the happiness and peace and hope in his own heart for this world and the world to come. He knew that life meant deeper and nobler things than ever entered these men's hearts to conceive.

Do you wonder that he impressed them favourably ? Do you wonder that they should feel as they went back to their palace, this fanatic is at least a real man ? that Agrippa should say to Festus as he departed, " We could set him at liberty to-day if he had not appealed unto Cæsar."

So Paul went back to his prison to prepare for his voyage, and the governor went to his office to write his report to Rome, whose favourable tenor we may well believe had much to do with Paul's acquittal in his first trial before Nero.

CHAPTER XVIII

THE SHIPWRECK

WE have now come to that portion of St. Luke's
Diary known to us as the 27th chapter of the Acts of
the Apostles, " the sailors' chapter," which Nelson
studied on his flagship the morning of the Trafalgar
fight. It is suggested that Luke must have been a
sailor or a ship's doctor before Paul first met him in
the harbour of Troas. For sailors say that no lands-
man could have written so accurate a sea story.

I

A.D. 60. A late September morning in the harbour
of Cæsarea, with the sun flashing on the pikes and
helmets of Roman soldiers. They are a troop of the
Augustan Regiment—the " King's Own " as we should
say—drawn up on the quay surrounding a group of
prisoners in chains. Paul is one of the prisoners. As
a Roman citizen on appeal to the Emperor he is,
doubtless, a man of some distinction amongst the other
prisoners, many of whom, when they get to Rome, will
probably be flung to the lions in the arena.

Julius, the centurion, is in charge of the escort. A
kindly man is Julius the centurion, and a good friend
to Paul. He has got to know him well during his

imprisonment. He was probably one of the guard of honour when Agrippa and Bernice heard that generous appeal, " I wish to God that you were all such as I am—except these bonds." One would like to know whether Paul's religion appealed to Julius the centurion.

There is a coasting ship of Adramytium waiting at the side. Soon the centurion has his charge on board, and Paul is at last started towards his goal of many years—to Rome. He knew he must go some time, since the Lord had willed it, but how little he expected to accomplish it like this—in chains.

Not that he would face it gloomily. Paul was no pessimist. He knew it was God's leading. He knew he was in God's care. He longed to see the Imperial City, and hoped to accomplish something for his Master there in the world's centre. He had an interesting and exciting adventure before him which would bring him face to face with the emperor of the known world. True, it might end in death. But that only meant a still more interesting and exciting adventure in that wondrous Life of the Hereafter. And besides, what would mean a good deal to Paul, he was not alone. Luke, " the beloved physician " and friend, was with him, and another old friend, Aristarchus, from Macedonia. We see from his Roman epistle that he had many friends in that city. We see too, in that epistle, that he had sent salutations to his old comrades Aquila and Priscilla. So he would expect that dear old couple also to meet him in Rome.

Things were not so bad, after all, in spite of fetters and dangers. There is always a bright side to a Christian man's troubles. With his friendships and hopes and his sense of God's presence and the quiet confidence with which he looks on death, the world has little power to keep men like Paul gloomy.

II

Next day they reach Sidon, and Julius the centurion courteously treated Paul and sent him ashore on parole to visit his friends. A week later they reach Myra, where a great Alexandrian grain ship is at the wharf overtopping all the shipping in the harbour. This exactly suits the plans of the centurion, for the ship is one of the Egyptian grain fleet bound for Italy. Egypt, for many years, was one of the chief granaries of the Empire, and this is evidently one of the Government transports. So, notwithstanding the crowd already on board, Julius exercises his right as a Government officer and promptly tranships his company.

Better, perhaps, had he been less prompt, for the grainship is clumsy and heavily laden, and the time of the winter storms is near. They are uneasy from the beginning. They start out on an ugly sea. They lumber along for many days hugging the shore, and when at last they have to venture out into the open they are glad to take refuge soon in the Cretan port of Fair Havens.

Now they have to make a serious decision. It is death to venture into the raging storm outside. There is a strong feeling in favour of lying up where they are for the winter. But the captain of the ship thinks he can creep along the coast to Phenice, where there is a safer harbour, though at the risk of being blown out to sea. They never got to Phenice. When the south wind blew softly, the captain made his venture. But that " south wind blowing softly " played the traitor. Out beyond the headlands they see the coming tempest. In an hour the Euroclydon is upon them, sweeping down from the Cretan hills, threatening to blow the ship out of the water, and there is a treacherous rock-bound shore on the lee. So there is nothing for it but to run out into the open and scud before the gale.

Then came a terrible time, never to be forgotten, when even the most experienced sailors abandoned hope. Luke writes in his diary : " All hope that we should be saved was taken away." The pressure on the great central mast wrenched the whole frame-work of the ship, and the pumps could not keep down the water in the hold. This was the chief danger in ships of that period, and in the midst of the mad storm they had to attempt the only remedy. They passed ropes under the keel undergirding the ship to prevent further opening of the seams. But it availed them little. The leaks gained on them. In desperation they threw out all they could to lighten the ship, and the next day they threw over all the spare gear.

Then followed days of dark despair. Literally dark, for the sky above them was black as ink and neither sun nor stars for many days appeared, and still the storm howled and the huge ship was flung about helpless on the waves.

It is an awful thing to know that death is sweeping down upon you hour by hour, to hear it coming with its hideous thunder, and yet, in the darkness, to see nothing of your danger nor of the way out. There was no mariner's compass in those days—only the sun and stars to guide. They could take no observations of sun by day or stars by night. They knew not where the reefs were or the rockbound shore. Nerves were tightly on the strain. Any moment might mean death. And there were 276 people crowded together in the darkness and wet and bitter cold waiting for the end. So tense was the strain that they took no meals for days together. No one who has not been through such a time can realise what it meant.

III

In the midst of it all stood one man confident and calm. Not merely brave. There were other brave men on that ship who could die without whining about it. There are many brave men, thank God, even without religion, as the stories of the Great War abundantly testify. And I think bravery, even without religion, is a fine thing in God's sight. Finer, at any rate, than cowardice without religion.

But confidence and calm at such times is a different thing, and for that one wants God. That only comes from consciousness of God's presence and God's love to all His poor children. That was what gave Paul the unshaken nerves, the steady hand, the heart beating evenly. He had been in three shipwrecks already. A night and a day he had tossed in the deep clinging to a spar. He had faced furious crowds and scourging and stoning. Now he seems facing certain death by drowning. And still his face is calm and his heart is brave, strengthened with God's presence in the inner man. Life had no terrors for the man who felt

Christ beside him. Death had no fear for one who desired " to depart and be with Christ which is far better."

IV

That is set before us here as the attitude of a Christian man facing death. Do you feel that it is too high an ideal, that you could never reach that life of calm? I feel the same—and yet I think we are wrong. Paul's secret was that he lived much in prayer and communion with God. Here in the midst of this terrified uproar I read that he found time for prayer and intercourse with his Lord, and that somehow assurance came to him that all would be well.

You know as well as I—however little we may profit by it—that there is no other such help in the troubles of life as the habit of getting some little time at least every day to withdraw into the holy mount with God. The men who in every age have done most to brighten life and lift the world towards God have been the men who lived thus. It is only they who can really witness to the value of it. And they would all tell you, with Paul, that prayer means power, that prayer means victory, that prayer means peace and calm. They could not do without it. Paul could not do without it. The Lord Himself could not do without it. Away from the troubles and disappointments of earth he would retire into the lonely mountain to continue all night in prayer and communion with the Father. Both Paul and his Lord are continually exhorting us to this secret of peace and calm. Perhaps we can never get into the heights, but could we not do a little better than we are doing to win the habit of running to God like little children and telling Him things and being calmed by His presence ?

V

Then we should be able to cheer and hearten other people as Paul did. From his communion with God he comes to that frightened crowd. " Cheer up ! Be of good cheer ! Take you food and strengthen your hearts, for I have the assurance from God, whose I am and whom I serve, that all will be well."

I call your attention to that picture of Paul cheering up those troubled people. " Cheer up ! Be of good cheer ! " That familiar phrase of Jesus should express the ministry of every Christian man and woman. It is your business, every one of you. You are not all called to the ministry of preaching, but you are all called to the ministry of cheering and heartening up your poor comrades in this troubled world. They want it badly ; never, perhaps, more than in these days after the War. God wants you to " hearten up " people. If you have your own troubles keep them to yourself. Keep a bright face. Wag your tail even if things are hard with you. That itself is a help and it is pleasing to God.

But you say that Paul had a divine assurance that all would be well. Well, have you not a similar assurance to give ? Even in life's big troubles God has given to us, as to St. Paul, assurance that should cheer men's hearts. We can tell the man miserable about his past life of the forgiveness of sins. Even in the worst troubles—even to the mother whose boy has died in battle, we can tell of God's revelation, of the wondrous new adventure into which her young soldier has gone in the great Life of the Hereafter. Let us do our part every one of us to help this poor world to "be of good cheer."

VI

See how those troubled people respond to Paul's hopefulness. Sailors in times of danger are readiest of all men to believe in intervention from another world. They feel that this man is in touch with God. So they take their food and their nerves grow calmer to face, with new courage, what is still before them.

They need all their courage for the last terrible night. At midnight there is a cry of "Land ahead!" They can hear the sound of the breakers and see the angry line of white, an awful sight when you cannot tell what is in front. So they sounded and found it twenty fathoms, and in a few moments more it is fifteen fathoms. They see the end is near. They dare not cast anchors from the bow lest the ship should swing round to the rocks. Desperately they cast out four anchors from the stern and long for the day. Whatever is before them they can do nothing more now.

While they wait in the darkness Paul hears whisperings and surreptitious movements. The hour of danger shews up dastards as well as heroes. The sailors are trying to lower a boat and escape. He whispers to the centurion, and in a moment the Roman sword has severed the rope, and the empty boat is gone.

But there is a danger closer to him. As the centurion turns his officer salutes him, " Sir, shall we execute the prisoners lest they escape ? " It says much for the fine discipline of the soldiers that they should think of this terrible duty at such a crisis. But Julius thinks of Paul, to whom the whole ship's company owes so much. They could not afford to let Paul die. So he takes it on himself to forbid the execution.

At last came the dawn. Right in front is a break in the rocks and a sandy cove. " Cut the anchor ropes. Let her drift ashore ! " But a cross current caught the ship and flung her broadside to the sea. And the waves leap on her, they fling her on the rocks, they tear her to pieces. In the wild confusion each man grasps what floating thing he can, and crushed and bleeding they were flung upon the shore. God was caring as He cares for all of us whether there be a Paul amongst us or not.

Perhaps you will remind me that He often lets us drown. Even so. Even when He lets us be drowned and swept into the Unseen. He is caring none the less. He is at the other side waiting. " And so, some on boards and some on broken pieces of the ship, they all escaped safe to land."

CHAPTER XIX

IN CHAINS

THUS ends another crisis in the life of Paul. As we close the story one cannot help feeling what a pity Luke was not with him all the time. What a life of exciting adventure we should hear of if we could have the whole stirring story thus graphically told, instead of having to content ourselves with the bare passing mention of the days that Paul had in his memory before he met his biographer or when the biographer was away.

I fear Paul must have been a very silent, unsatisfactory companion to the man who was writing the story of his life. In the quiet days on shipboard, in the four prison years when they were so much together, what things he could have told, and how well Luke could have recorded them. I wonder if Luke ever saw that tantalising reference to earlier days in the Corinthian letters?

Of the Jews five times received I forty stripes save one. Three times was I beaten with rods, once was I stoned, three times I suffered shipwreck, a night and a day I have been in the deep, in journeyings often, in perils of rivers, in perils of robbers, in perils from my countrymen, in perils from the Gentiles, in perils in the city, in perils in the wilderness, in perils in the sea, in perils among false brethren, in labour and travail, in watchings often, in hunger and thirst and fastings, and cold and nakedness (2 Cor. xi., 24).

What a stirring narrative that would have made in the hands of a man who has told so graphically the story of the shipwreck.

But I suppose Paul did not care to talk about himself, except when it was necessary in talking about his Lord. The mysterious Presence in which he lived dwarfed all else for him. I can picture the silent man looking out over the sea as memory played over those pictures in the panorama of his life, and tracing more and more the Guiding Hand, even where he had not seen it at the time. And I can imagine what an interesting vision will be our own life-pictures, by and bye, when we see them in memory from the life beyond, and see God always in the midst, though we knew it not.

II

That shipwrecked company found themselves on the island which we call Malta. The place is almost certainly identified in what is now called St. Paul's Bay. The " barbarous people " showed them no little kindness, and Paul responded to their kindness by healing the sick, and telling the people his joyous gospel of hope. We can conjecture what three months of such ministry must have meant to the Maltese.

III

Three months later.

Italy is in sight. The winter is over. On the shores of the lovely bay of Naples the land is putting on its spring mantle of green. In the fine harbour of Puteoli, the Liverpool of ancient Italy, sailors on the crowded wharves are cheering the entrance of the first Alexandrian grain ship of the season, the Castor and Pollux. She sails in proudly with topsails set, the privilege only of Alexandrian grain ships. She is carrying the bread of life for Italy—carrying also, in a deeper sense, the Bread of Life for the world, for Paul and his ship-wrecked company are on board. She has picked them up at Malta on her way.

We have a picture in Roman history of another Alexandrian grain ship coming into this same harbour of Puteoli a few years earlier. Before her in the bay lay the royal barge carrying the dying Emperor Augustus. The sailors on the grain ship crowded the yards to cheer him, and with garlands and incense they worshipped their emperor as a god. The religion of ancient Italy reached no higher than that, the worship of a dying conqueror.

The herald of a great Conqueror was coming in now, but no one took any notice. The world had not grown better since Augustus' day. The Emperor was still the representative of the Divine. Roman society was rotten to the core. These lovely villas on the bay were homes of profligacy and lust, of unnatural vices, and filthy abominations, such as cannot be mentioned here. In one of these villas the man who was now emperor had killed his own mother.

Just a year later, when Paul was in Rome, this same emperor, the representative of the Divine, put his young wife to death, and sent her head to his adulterous mistress, Poppea, and divine honours were paid to the adulteress and her baby. Such was the condition of the world before Christianity came. And sometimes, even now, both in war and peace times, the newspapers give us ugly reminders of what we might drop back to again if we let our religion slip.

It was the most beautiful scene on earth that Paul looked on that morning from the deck of the Castor and Pollux. But, oh ! it sorely needed Paul's message —it sorely needed Christ.

IV

There were Christians to meet him even in Puteoli. Curious in what unexpected places these Christians seem turning up. We hear nothing of any missionaries sent to Italy. But that seed of the Kingdom has a strange power of spreading.

Julius the centurion has to hasten on his company on the great Appian road to Rome, crowded all day long with the varied traffic between Puteoli and the imperial city. No doubt there were stirring sights on that march, but our historian is only interested in the dirty little town of Apii Forum, on the way, at the end of the canal, with its motley population of mule drivers and tavern keepers and drunken bargemen. For there Paul first meets the brethren from the city, come to meet him. Some he knows personally, others only by hearsay. We have a list of his friends to whom he sends salutations in his Epistle to the Romans.

It was pleasant to meet them all, but I fancy his heart stirring with a deeper pleasure as he sees amongst them the dear old faces of Aquila and Priscilla, those old comrades of his, laughing in the delight of meeting him again. And I read, " he thanked God and took courage."

V

Now from the shoulder of the Alban hills he gets his first view of the Eternal City. He has seen many fine cities in his time, but nothing like this. Glorious, beautiful Rome, with all her historic associations, the incarnation of earthly power, the mistress of the world ! His friends point out the Capitol and the Imperial Palace, the countless temples and the stately triumphal arches, commemorating the Empire's glories, the vast Circus Maximus on the left, where every year 10,000 victims died, butchered to make a Roman holiday, in that old world without Christ.

Now they are in the city. On through the narrow streets they march, amid ever-increasing throngs of people, till the weary soldiers halt at last at the barracks of the Prætorian Guard, and Julius the centurion surrenders his prisoners. And here begin the two or more long years of Paul's imprisonment in Rome.

VI

Like his time in Cæsarea it seems to have been made as easy as possible for him. Julius the centurion would be sure to speak well of him to the officers of the guard. " He is a splendid fellow, this Paul. We owe much to him on this journey. You can trust him to the uttermost. If you were even to parole him on his own simple promise you would be perfectly safe. Such men as he could not lie to you. Be as good to him as you can."

And so, instead of languishing in the Prætorian dungeons, he was allowed to live outside in his own hired lodging with the soldier that guarded him, and with free leave to see and communicate with his friends.

Evidently Paul's circumstances must have improved in his old age, since he, who had to work for his daily bread on his missionary tours, could now afford to live in his own hired dwelling and support himself. It is suggested that his father had died and his family inheritance had come to him, which seems a fairly probable conjecture.

So I read " he abode two whole years in his own hired dwelling . . . teaching the things concerning the Lord Jesus Christ with all boldness, no man forbidding him."

VII

These are the last words in the Acts of the Apostles. Here St. Luke's diary suddenly fails us. Why? Surely Luke did not mean to leave his hero there in prison with his trial pending. We know that Luke was with him. One feels sure that another book was intended to complete the biography. But we have not got it. Probably it was never finished. It may be that Luke lost his life in the terrible persecution which caught his master later on, and that

the rest of his diary, for which the world would give
so much to-day, was flung out unnoticed on a Roman
rubbish heap.

So we have to go on now without his guidance.
We have the traditions of the early Church, but they
do not carry us far. Fortunately we have the letters
which the Apostle wrote during his imprisonment,
and on these we have largely to depend for the rest
of his story.

From these letters we gather that even with all
his privileges it was not a pleasant time. The letters
refer frequently to his chains and his bonds. "The
soldier that guarded him" may seem a small matter.
But put yourself in his place. Think of the intolerable
infliction of being chained all the time to another, a
heathen soldier, often a brutal, beastly sort of man.
We read that in the imprisonment of King Agrippa I.
in Rome, the Prætorian prefect was bribed to secure
that the soldiers chained to him should be decent,
good-tempered men. The guard would be relieved
twice a day, but Paul had no relief—no privacy.
I read lately of a mediæval tyrant chaining two men
together for months as a distressing punishment.

But Paul had to get used to it. And I think he
did more, that he made his guards like him. You see,
the duty would not be very irksome to them for a
few hours at a time. They could not help admiring
the high character and kindly disposition of their
prisoner. I can well believe that some of them grew
attached to him; that little groups of them off duty
would drop in and talk to him in the evenings. And
Paul could not be long in intercourse with any man
without helping him towards higher things. They

often chatted to each other in barracks about their prisoner and his religion. And he is quite pleased at this. He tells the Philippians in a letter of this period " the things that have happened to me have turned out for the furtherance of the gospel, for my bonds in Christ have become manifest throughout the whole Prætorian guard." We gather that some of them became faithful disciples of Christ, for he writes in the same letter : " The Christian brethren that are here salute you, especially those that are of Cæsar's household," who would probably be the Prætorian lifeguards. When one thinks how many soldiers would come in close touch with him in the continual change of the guard during two years, one can imagine the difference it would make in that regiment.

VIII

One day, just after his arrival, he invited some of the chief Jews of the city to meet him, but the interview was very unsatisfactory. The Roman Christians were, of course, his most frequent visitors. You can well believe that his presence in that prison room deepened the whole life of that Christian community. Many a poor sinner would come to him in his trouble. Many a poor presbyter would come to consult him and talk about Jesus, and go back to his congregation with his spirit stirred to preach to them the next Sunday as he had never preached before.

But we learn from the epistles of this period that his sphere of action spread far beyond these. Even in his Roman prison there still lay upon him " the care of all the churches." He still watched over his distant converts. And for this he had to keep around him his faithful band of friends, who should travel to and fro, and keep him in touch with them.

He tells us that Luke was with him, and Tychicus, his old companion in travel, and young Timothy, his " beloved son in the faith," dearest and closest of them all, associated with him even in the writing of his epistles. And with especial interest we read that John Mark was with him. You remember young Mark, who had deserted when Paul and Barnabas were on their first missionary journey, and who was the cause of that unhappy separation between him and Barnabas. Paul was very angry with him then, and refused to let him go with them any more. Therefore it is very interesting to find him helping him now and to see how much Paul had grown to care for him.

CHAPTER XX

LETTERS FROM ROME

VISITORS often came, too, from these far-off congregations. All roads led to Rome. Members of these congregations had often to come to the city on business, and, of course, would come to see him and bring him affectionate messages and perhaps little comforts for his prison life. And Paul would send back his greetings and sometimes send important letters.

You remember Philippi, where he had been scourged so cruelly and where the Philippian jailer had been converted in the dungeon. One day an old friend from Philippi arrived. His name was Epaphroditus, and we judge from expressions about him that he was much beloved in the Church. Probably he was one of their presbyters. For all that we know he may have been the converted jailer. All the old friends, Lydia and the rest, sent their love and they also sent him a present. The old man was greatly touched. He loved his Philippian people better than any other and he thought much about them in the coming weeks, for Epaphroditus fell sick in Rome, " sick, nigh unto death," and the home people were anxious about him. They and Paul prayed earnestly to God. Prayer was a very real thing to Christians then. He must have been a close friend of Paul, judging from his relief at his recovery. " God had mercy on him," he writes, " and not on him but on me also lest I should have sorrow upon sorrow."

When Epaphroditus was convalescent, Paul wrote a letter to the Philippians which his friend should take home with him, the most beautiful and tender of all his epistles. And the most joyous. Out from the dreary prison room it came to the troubled Philippians and to despondent poor Christians all over the world since, telling of the inner gladness welling up in his heart. " I rejoice in the Lord." " Fulfil ye my joy." " Rejoice in the Lord always, and again I say, rejoice ! "

All down the ages we have countless such instances of the happiness which religion gives in the midst of troubles. And it is worth thinking of in these troubled days. It is hard to be cheery sometimes when clouds are resting on us. But God is near and God is caring, and it is wholesome for us to see what religion can do for men who are really living close to their Lord.

II

When you read this epistle put it in its right setting. Paul, writing or dictating it to Timothy, in his prison room with a soldier chained to him, and his sick friend waiting to carry the letter home. Let us glance over some of the little papyrus sheets as Timothy lays them down :

I thank my God upon all my remembrance of you, always making my supplication with joy for your fellowship in furtherance of the gospel from the first day until now. . . . For God is my witness how I long after you all in the tender mercies of Christ Jesus. And this I pray, that your love may abound yet more and more . . . that ye may approve the things that are excellent, that ye may be sincere and void of offence unto the day of Christ, being filled with the fruits of righteousness which are through Jesus Christ unto the glory and praise of God.

Do not be troubled about me. The things which have happened to me have fallen out unto the furtherance of the gospel through the whole Prætorian guard and through the brethren here, who have grown abundantly bold to speak the word of God without fear.

And do not trouble about the result of my trial. I think I shall be acquitted, but what matters so that Christ be magnified in me whether by life or by death. For me to live is Christ, to die is gain. Either alternative is good. I hardly know which I should choose. To depart and be with Christ would be better for me, to abide in the flesh would be better for you. And I believe I shall abide and meet you again. Only let your life be worthy of the gospel of Christ, that whether I come to you or not I may know that ye stand fast in the Lord.

Now be careful about those little disagreements among you.

If there is any comfort in Christ, if any consolation of love, if any fellowship of the Spirit, fulfil ye my joy having the same love, doing nothing through strife or vainglory, but in lowliness of mind, each counting other better than himself, not looking each to his own things, but each also to the things of others. Have this mind in you which was also in Christ Jesus.

Even if I am to be offered as a sacrifice, I joy and rejoice with you all as you do with me.

I hope to send Timothy shortly to you that I may be of good comfort when I know your state. For ye know that as a child with his father he has served with me in the furtherance of the gospel. But I trust in the Lord that I myself also shall come to you shortly.

I send back Epaphroditus, your friend and your minister to my need. He has been very sick, nigh unto death, but

H

God had mercy on him and on me also, lest I should have sorrow upon sorrow. Receive him in the Lord with all joy and hold such men in honour always.

Rejoice in the Lord always, and again I say rejoice. Whatever happens rejoice in the Lord. I count all things but loss for the excellency of the knowledge of Christ Jesus my Lord. . . . One thing I do, forgetting the things that are behind and stretching forward to the things that are before, I press toward the mark for the prize of the high calling of God in Christ Jesus.

Finally, brethren, think high thoughts. Whatsoever things are true, whatsoever things are honourable, whatsoever things are just, whatsoever things are pure, whatsoever things are honourable and lovely and of good report, think on these things.

I am greatly pleased at your kind thought of me in sending your gift. Not that I speak in respect of want, for I have learned in whatsoever state I am therein to be content. But now I have all things and abound having received from Epaphroditus this gift that came from you. And my God shall supply all your need according to His riches in Christ Jesus. Give my love to all the friends. The brethren here send their greetings to you, especially those that are of Cæsar's household. The grace of the Lord Jesus Christ be with your spirit.

III

Amongst the many visitors to Paul in his prison room came one day a young runaway slave, named Onesimus. He had run away from his master at Colossæ, and we suspect, from a reference in Paul's epistle later, had stolen money from him. He had made for the great city to hide himself and to have a good time. A big city is the safest of all hiding places.

But one day someone brought him to see Paul. Or,
perhaps, the poor, hunted lad remembered Paul as a
visitor in old days at his master's house. For his
master, Philemon, was one of Paul's old converts.
He was a member of the Colossian church, and he
and his good wife, Apphia, were close friends of the
apostle, the sort of friends to whom you can write and
offer yourself for a visit without waiting for an invita-
tion. " You might get a room ready for me," Paul
writes to him, " as I hope, through God's blessing,
to come soon and visit you." It is only to very
intimate friends that you can write like that.

Paul's heart warmed to the young slave. Young
men had always a special attraction for him, and this
young scamp must have had something very winning
about him in spite of his wickedness. For there grew
a very close friendship between them. And Onesimus
became penitent and became a disciple of Christ.

IV

It is sometimes an awkward thing to become a
Christian. For you feel impelled to do the right thing,
which is so often a very unpleasant thing. The
religion which Paul taught was very practical.
Onesimus must not merely tell God that he is sorry, he
must go back to his master and confess and take his
punishment and make what restitution he can.

Some of us think it all right if we just tell God
that we are sorry. That is a very easy thing to do,
for we feel that God knows it already. Confession
does not bring any awkward consequences. I once
asked a small boy whether he had confessed to God a

certain sin. " Yes," he said. And then he made me smile as he added, " You see, I don't mind telling God, because He won't tell anybody." Have not you often felt like that ? Repentance means more than that. It means earnest resolve for the future, also restitution, where possible, and willingness to take the unpleasant consequences. That was what Paul taught his convert. " You must go back, my lad, and do the right, though it will be very hard for you to go and very hard for me to part with you. But I will write a note to my old friend to take with you."

So he sends back Onesimus with this note in his pocket and, fortunately, Philemon kept the note, and I suppose he gave it afterwards to the Colossian church to preserve with Paul's epistles.

It is a very interesting little page of the Bible. No formal teaching or disquisition on doctrines, but just a little impromptu letter dashed off at the moment. But it gives a glimpse into the heart of the writer, better than some more formal epistles. And it is a valuable illustration of the way in which Christianity deals with social problems, slavery and war and such like.

Slavery was an unutterably cruel institution. The man, the woman, the young girl, the child belonged to the master to do what he liked with. This very year of Paul's arrival in Rome the prefect of the city was killed by the slave lover of one of his slave girls. Probably he deserved killing. In revenge for it the whole body of his 400 slaves, men, women, and children, were put to death. How did Christianity deal with slavery ? Not by stirring up rebellion or rousing slaves to insurrection, but by gradually leavening society with the spirit of that religion which recognised all as brethren and as equal in the sight of the Father of us all. " Onesimus," writes Paul to the master of this young slave, " Onesimus is my friend and a disciple of your Lord and mine. Receive him as a brother." " Masters," he writes in the Ephesian epistle, " be good to your slaves, for their Master and yours is in Heaven and there is no respect of persons with Him." That is the spirit of the religion of Jesus, and when it grew sufficiently strong in the world, slavery was swept away for ever.

That, too, is how wars will be swept away. That is God's method. Not by paralysing the aggressor or smiting him with fire from heaven, but by gradually permeating life with the religion which makes all men brothers. God's plan is slow but it is sure, like the incoming of the tide. It is slow because its appeal is to individual wills, and everyone who yields his life to it is hastening that coming day when men will look back on war with the shame with which they now look back on slavery.

v

Here is the letter which Onesimus brought to his master and from which you can gather the whole of his story :

Paul, a prisoner of Jesus Christ and Timothy our brother, to Philemon our beloved and to Apphia our sister and to Archippus and the church in thy house. . . . I thank my God always making mention of you in my prayers. For I had much joy and comfort in your love, because the hearts of the saints have been refreshed through you, my brother.

Wherefore, though I might enjoin you to do what is fitting, yet for love's sake I rather beseech you being such a one as Paul the aged and now a prisoner of Jesus Christ. I beseech you for my child Onesimus, whom I have begotten in my bonds. . . . whom I send back to you though I fain would have kept him with me that in your behalf he might minister to me in the bonds of the gospel, but without your mind I would do nothing, that your goodness should not be of necessity but of free will.

For perhaps he was parted from you for a season that you might have him for ever, no longer as a bondservant but as a brother, beloved . . . If then you count me as a partner, receive him as myself. If he has wronged you or owes you anything put it down to my account. I, Paul, write with my own hand I will repay it. Though indeed you owe to me even your own soul. . . . Having confidence in your obedience I write, knowing that you will do even beyond what I say.

But withal prepare me also a lodging, for I hope through your prayers I shall be granted to come to you.

Epaphras, my fellow-prisoner in Christ Jesus, salutes you, and so do Mark and Anistarchus and Demas and Luke, my fellow-workers. The grace of our Lord Jesus Christ be with your spirit.

CHAPTER XXI

LETTERS FROM ROME—*Continued*

BUT before Onesimus started for Colossæ there was occasion for another letter to be sent to the church in his home town. There had arrived in Rome another Colossian, either the founder or an important presbyter of the Colossian church. His name was Epaphras. He consulted with Paul about some difficulties that had arisen. It seems that a travelling preacher had come teaching Christianity, but a Christianity mixed up with some queer notions of Rabbinical theology and Greek philosophy—about the worship of angels, and the necessity of an extremely ascetic life, and other errors. The danger was that it looked so like Christianity. Just as if a Christian Science teacher, for example, should preach his Christianity to us.

So Paul decided to write an epistle to the Colossians and send it by Tychicus, one of his associates, who should also take charge of young Onesimus on his way home. From the letter it is evident that Paul did not know the Colossians personally, and perhaps was not very clear about the false teaching either. He had to go on what Epaphras told him.

I omit the synopsis of this Colossian letter as I

want to keep your attention fresh for the following epistle, where some of its best thoughts are even better expressed. Two sentences, however, I quote with a special purpose. "All my affairs shall Tychicus make known unto you—I send him to you, together with Onesimus, the faithful and beloved brother, who is one of yourselves." "Give my salutations to the brethren in Laodicea, and when this epistle has been read among you, cause that it also be read in the church of the Laodiceans and ye also read the epistle that I am sending to Laodicea."

II

So the two messengers start for Colossæ, Tychicus to present his epistle to the church, Onesimus to face the master whom he had wronged, carrying with him his precious letter of apology Here we regretfully bid Onesimus farewell. We should like to know how he turned out afterwards, for Paul had a great belief in the lad. History tells of a bishop of Berea named Onesimus, and some think that he was the former slave. It is only a conjecture.

But Tychicus had another letter to carry, and thereby hangs a tale. We have seen that Paul speaks of an epistle to the Laodiceans which he was sending at the same time. Now we have in the Bible no epistle with that title, wherefore many have concluded that it is lost. But we have an extremely important one called the Epistle to the Ephesians. It is rather puzzling, since it has none of the personal references which we should expect in a letter to people whom he knew so well for three years and amongst whom he had such an exciting time. It might have been written to any church. The personal element is quite absent. Some passages look as if he had only a hearsay knowledge of the people. One is inclined to doubt if it was really addressed to the Ephesians.

In addition to this we have statements from several ancient fathers of the Church that the manuscripts of this epistle which they had, omitted the word Ephesus in the inscription. The two oldest copies in existence to-day bear this out. One is in Petrograd and one in the Vatican library at Rome. They have no title. And finally we have a testimony that, in some places at least, it was known as the Epistle to the Laodiceans. Yet there must be some good reason for the fact that the title " Ephesians " always clung to it in Church tradition.

III

The question is not worth discussing further. I believe it was a general Pastoral letter for Ephesus and Laodicea and other churches—if so, it was the greatest Pastoral ever written. I call your attention now to the Epistle to the Ephesians. It is Paul's last and noblest letter to the Gentile churches. Here he is at his best and greatest. He passes away and rises far above all the (necessary) lower controversies of other epistles about Jews and Gentiles and ceremonial rites and systems of theology. He rises into the sublime and the infinite. His imagination is peopled with things in the heavenly places, his fancy is rapt into visions of God before the world was. To many devout students this epistle represents the high-water mark of Paul's inspired thought after his four prison years of contemplation of the stupendous mystery of God's dealings with man.

IV

First comes the tremendous thought of God's Divine purpose from the beginning before anything was made that was made. This Church of Christ, he says, is no accident, no afterthought. It was the eternal purpose of God's love before the foundation of the world that the eternal Christ should save humanity, that evil should be swept out of the Universe for ever. That the poor children should be gathered into the arms of the Father, that God should be all in all.

Blessed be the God and Father of our Lord Jesus Christ, who blessed us with all spiritual blessings in heavenly places in Christ, as He hath chosen us in Him before the foundation of the world, having predestined us unto the adoption of children by Jesus Christ, according to the good pleasure of His grace wherein He hath made us accepted in the Beloved, in whom we have redemption through His blood even the forgiveness of sins. . . . that in the dispensation of the fulness of times He might gather unto one all things in Christ, according to His purpose who worketh all things after the counsel of His own will.

" I want you to know," he says, " this wondrous plan of God's everlasting purpose of love." I pray that the God and Father of Our Lord Jesus Christ the Father of glory, may give unto you the spirit of wisdom and revelation in the knowledge of Him ; the eyes of your understanding being enlightened that you may know the hope of His calling and the riches and glory of this inheritance, and the exceeding greatness of His power toward us who believe, according to the working of His mighty power, which He wrought in Christ when He raised Him from the dead and set Him at His own right hand far above all principality and power and might and dominion, and hath put all things under His feet, and gave Him to be head of all things to the Church, which is His Body. See how this plan of God is working out.

Even you Gentiles come into this loving purpose. who were aliens from the commonwealth of Israel, having no hope and without God in the world. Now you who were far off are made nigh by the blood of Christ. Now ye are no more strangers and foreigners, but fellow-citizens with the saints and of the household of God, built upon the foundations of the apostles and prophets, Jesus Christ Himself being the chief corner stone.

God has allowed even me, the poor prisoner of Jesus Christ, to understand and teach this mystery which in other ages was not made known to the sons of men. To me who am the least of all saints was this grace given that I should preach among the Gentiles the unsearchable riches of Christ, and to make men see this mystery which from the beginning hath been hid in God . . . according to the eternal purpose which He purposed in Christ Jesus our Lord. For this cause I bow my knees to the Father of our Lord Jesus Christ, that He would grant you that ye being rooted and grounded in love may be able to comprehend this mystery, that ye may be able to comprehend with all saints what is the breadth and length and depth and height of that love of Christ which passeth knowledge, that ye may be filled with all the fulness of God.

V

This is a brief and very imperfect résumé of the first half of the epistle. Even if there were time and if I understood him better, still it is not easy to express simply Paul's thought in this passage. For his thoughts are deep. And his style is difficult. One of his sentences here is like a German sentence, twelve verses long. But perhaps I have given you at least some little glimpse of the awe and wonder and adoring gratitude with which he contemplates this mystery of God's eternal purpose of love to men, before the time when " in the beginning God created the heavens and the earth."

Now, in the beginning of the fourth chapter, he turns straight to the practical conclusion from all this with the word " therefore." Because of God's love and God's care and God's thought for you from the eternities.

Therefore, I, Paul, the prisoner of the Lord, beseech you to walk worthy of the vocation wherewith ye are called." That is the keynote of his appeal.

Therefore, keep unbroken the unity of the Church, one Lord, one Faith, one Baptism, one God and Father of all, who is above all and through all and in you all.

Therefore, walk no longer as other Gentiles walk in the vanity of their mind. Put off the old man which waxeth corrupt and put on the new man which, after God, hath been created in righteousness and true holiness.

Therefore, putting away falsehood, speak every man truth with his neighbours. Let him that stole steal no more. Let no corrupt communication proceed out of your mouth. Let all bitterness and wrath and anger be put away from you and be ye kind to one another, tender-hearted, forgiving one another, even as God for Christ's sake hath forgiven you.

Therefore, be ye imitators of God as dear children and walk in love, even as Christ also loved you and gave Himself for you.

Ye were once darkness but are now light in the Lord. Walk as children of the light and have no fellowship with the unfruitful works of darkness.

Keep your family life as God would have it. Wives, be subject to your husbands. Husbands, love your wives even as Christ loved the Church. Children, obey your parents in the Lord. Servants, be obedient to your masters, not with eye service as men-pleasers but as servants of Christ, doing your service as to the Lord not unto men. And ye masters, do the same by them, knowing that both their Master and yours is in Heaven and there is no respect of persons with Him.

Finally, be strong in the Lord and in the power of His might. Put on the whole armour of God that ye may be able to stand in the evil day.

And continue in supplication for all Christians and for me that utterance may be given to me to make known with boldness this mystery of the gospel for which I am an ambassador in a chain.

Peace be to the brethren and love with faith from God the Father and the Lord Jesus Christ. Grace be with all them that love the Lord Jesus Christ in sincerity.

VI

These are the four Epistles of the Captivity, Philippians, Colossians, Ephesians, Philemon, some of the results of Paul's two years in that prison room. Which suggests a lesson for us. To many of Paul's friends it must have seemed such a waste that God should leave His great apostle cooped up in confinement for two years, when he might have been preaching Christ and building up in the Imperial City the central church of Christendom.

We, looking back on the results to-day can hardly feel like that. Perhaps it was worth while, in order that Christ's gospel should get a hold in the Roman army who went to all parts of the world, who probably had much to do with first bringing that gospel to Britain. Surely it was worth while to give Paul time to think. Surely these four Epistles of the Captivity were of more value to the Church than would be two years' preaching in Rome. So St. John was exiled to lonely Patmos and wrote the Book of the Revelations. So Bunyan, kept twelve years in Bedford Jail, wrote his Pilgrim's Progress. So Luther, shut up in the Wartzburg, translated the New Testament for the Germans. (One wishes they had made better use of it.)

So, too, to some of ourselves it has seemed waste that we have been disappointed of certain promotions, that we have been relegated to an obscure position or set aside by ill-health from active work. It is not easy, but it is wise to say at such times, Let me take it as God's will. Let me culture my soul and help my neighbours and make happiness around me and leave the results with God. That was what Paul did and God took care of the results. God was guiding. God was loving. God was caring. Storm and shipwreck, soldier and fetter, Cæsarea and Rome, all worked out right for Paul in the end. These things that happened to me, he writes, have turned out all right for the furtherance of the Gospel.

Learn the lesson. Do not fret at the limitations and disabilities of your life. Rest in the Lord. If you are trying to live for Him, wherever you are placed, all things will work together for good to achieve God's ideal in you, to make you what in your best moments you long to become.

CHAPTER XXII

The Passing of Paul

After these weary years of the law's delay, at length, in the spring of A.D. 63, the trial came on. He stood at last before Nero's Court of Appeal. As he had anticipated in his letters the verdict was favourable. He was set free. Possibly the Jews had grown tired of pursuing him. The reports of Festus and Agrippa and the Chief Captain Lysias were in his favour. The kindly centurion, Julius, would help him all he could. The officers of the guard would say their good word for him. And in any case, Roman judges would not be much concerned about a charge which turned largely on mere Jewish superstitions. Therefore, though his biographer does not tell the story, we may accept the uncontradicted belief of the early Church, that he was set free from his chains and went out again in his closing days to finish the great work to which the Lord had called him that day long ago on the Damascus road.

II

He had a narrower escape than he knew. If his trial had been delayed a little longer, nothing, humanly speaking, could have saved him.

For in the July of the next year (A.D. 64), came the historic Great Fire of Rome, blazing for six days and nights and nearly destroying the city. And, just as in the Great Fire of London the mob charged the crime on the Roman Catholics, so now they charged it on the inoffensive Christians. Those who knew best had their dark suspicions of the half insane emperor, Nero, and he, for his own sake, was only too glad to encourage the slander against the Christian community. So the year after Paul's trial a Christian was about as safe in Rome as a mad dog. A fierce persecution arose. They were tortured and crucified. That devilish emperor covered living men and women with tar and burned them as torches to illuminate the gardens. The Roman historian, Tacitus, tells us that a great number of Christians perished.

However, that was a year ahead, and meantime Paul was far away from Rome closing up his life work. Now, more than ever, we miss that lost notebook of St. Luke. For, surely it had an interesting story of the old man's last years. Outside his own letters we have only vague tradition to guide us. But, fortunately for us, his three last letters remain, the Pastoral Epistles, as they are called, to Timothy and Titus. No one can read them without seeing that they belong to this period.

Beyond the hints in these letters we cannot trace his movements. We may fairly suppose that he followed his intention expressed in his recent letter to Philemon, that he visited Colossæ and stayed with Philemon and met young Onesimus again, that he made a great final visitation of the churches which he had founded, and confirmed their organisation for the years when he should be gone. There is some evidence that he sailed by the Marseilles shipping line and founded Christian churches as far west as Spain. But we know very little about these closing years of his life. The whole picture is vague and shadowy, wanting the lost notebook of St. Luke.

III

Somewhere in these journeyings he wrote his First Epistle to Timothy giving directions about the order and government of the church, the ordaining of clergy, and the rules of life which Timothy must prescribe to be observed by Christian people.

The time had come for Paul, as well as the other apostles, to think of laying down their work and appointing successors and leaving broad rules for the guidance of the church when they should have gone back to their Master. Paul was now a worn-out man in broken health approaching his seventieth year. The impetuous soul was wearing through the frail, delicate little body. He had had a very hard life. He had done stupendous work. He had suffered greatly in body and mind. He was still cordially hated by a good many people. He had pressing anxieties, growing heavier as he grew older, " the care of all the churches." He was tired out. It must have been a relief to pass on his work to others. It must have been with a restful feeling that he wrote a little later " The time of my departure is at hand."

In this preparation for the future he must divest himself of friends who are needed for important positions in the church. He must part from his life companion, Timothy, just when his old age most needed him. It was for both of them a sore parting. " I remember your tears," he writes to Timothy a year later.

He invested Timothy with authority over the church in Ephesus and the regions around, and soon afterwards he similarly appointed Titus to Crete. They were to ordain clergy to rule the Church, to do what we now call, and what the Church for eighteen hundred years has called, the work of a bishop. They were young for such positions. They would require advice and directions. They might, perhaps, need Paul's letters as credentials. So a few months after parting with him he wrote from Macedonia his First Epistle to Timothy :

IV

Paul, an apostle of Jesus Christ, unto Timothy my true child in the faith, grace, mercy and peace from God the Father and Our Lord Jesus Christ. . . . This charge I commend to thee my son Timothy, that thou fight the good fight holding faith and a good conscience, which some having thrust from them, have made shipwreck of the faith, of whom are Hymenæus and Alexander, whom I have delivered unto Satan that they may learn not to blaspheme.

I direct you how to act in the house of God the Church of the living God.

I exhort, therefore, first of all that supplications, prayers, intercessions, be made for all men—I direct how you are to enjoin men to behave in the church. I direct how women are to act.

Faithful is the saying, If a man desire the office of a bishop he desireth a good work. (The word " bishop " here is misleading to us. The Greek word EPISCOPOS means simply an overseer, one who presides. While the apostle lived it was used of presbyters who were overseers over congregations. But as the Apostles began to pass away, the name became restricted to the Chief Overseers, the successors of the Apostles, who were invested by them with authority to ordain and rule. So the name Bishop and the office continue ever since. But here the name is applied to the presbyters ordained by Timothy as overseers of congregations.)

The Apostle is directing him what sort of man to ordain— he must be blameless, the husband of one wife, not given to much wine, ruling his household well and having a good reputation outside. " Lay hands suddenly on no man. Be careful whom you ordain. And when you have ordained them, see that they are properly supported, for the labourer is worthy of his hire. Likewise the deacons must be men of high character."

Thus and thus must you behave towards the widows on the poor fund—towards the younger women, etc. Thus I direct with regard to the rich, to slaves, to false teachers. So he lays down his direction to the young bishop for his guidance in the church.

Then for his personal life. Keep thyself pure. Watch against the love of money. O man of God, flee from these things—follow after righteousness, godliness, faith, love, patience, meekness. Fight the good fight of faith. I charge thee in the sight of God and of Christ Jesus that thou keep the commandment without spot until the appearing of Our Lord Jesus Christ. O Timothy, guard that which is committed unto thy trust. Peace be with you.

So ends the first epistle to Timothy.

V

Soon afterwards Paul visited the churches of Crete with Titus. He could not stay long enough to do all that was needful in ordaining clergy and checking false teachers. So he had to leave Titus there in the same position and authority as Timothy at Ephesus. Titus was young for a bishop, and it would seem that his authority was questioned. So, later on, it was necessary to write to him also. It is not necessary here to comment on the epistle to Titus, as it is, in substance, very like that to Timothy.

VI

So Paul continued his tour from town to town, from church to church, setting things in order, bidding them good-bye, leaving them "sorrowing for the words which he had said that they should see his face no more."

Every month danger drew nearer. The rage against Christians had spread from Rome to the Provinces, and such a prominent leader could not be safe for long. He would have to steal in and out of towns, secretly, trusting the loyalty of the church people not to betray him. He had no lack of enemies, Jews and Gentiles. At last they got him. Some informer laid a charge against him. "Alexander, the coppersmith, shewed against me much evil by his accusation," * he writes before his death. Perhaps it was he. We do not

* The Greek verb here expresses this thought.

know and it does not matter. He could not have escaped anyway. So they arrested him, perhaps at Nicopolis where he meant to spend the winter, perhaps at Troas in the house of Carpus, where, in the hurry of departure, he left his old travelling cloak and his books and parchments, of which we shall hear again. It seems probable that to escape an unfair trial in the Provinces he again used his privilege of appealing to Cæsar. At any rate he was taken to Rome again to be tried.

VII

It was a lonely journey to Rome this time—not like the last. One and another of his friends either had been sent on missions or else had deserted him in his trouble. Luke remained with him.

And when he got to Rome there was no group of friends to meet him as before. It was as much as their lives were worth to be seen with him now. Dear old Aquila and Priscilla had fled to Ephesus. Most of the others had escaped somewhere from Rome. Demas forsook him. The men of Asia Minor, when they came to Rome on business, no longer called to see him. " They have all turned away from me," he says. One brave friend from Ephesus stands out in fine contrast. We gather that he was dead when Paul wrote about him. " The Lord grant mercy to the house of Onesiphorus, he was not ashamed of my chains, but when he was in Rome he sought me diligently and found me. May the Lord grant him mercy in the Great Day."

We gather, too, that his imprisonment this time was very strict. No lodging in his own hired apartment as before, but shut up close within prison walls. We hear nothing of preaching or conversing with friends. We hear no word of hope that he might some day be free and visit old friends again. He is a doomed man, no prospect but death. "The time of my departure is come."

VIII

We get one closing glimpse of him that goes to our heart in the Second Epistle to Timothy, so far as we know, his very last written words.

In the great crisis of life there is usually one friend whom, above all others, a man specially wants near him. With Paul it was Timothy. We remember how deeply he was attached to him. Ever since the day when he first met the lad in Lycaonia, living with his mother and grandmother on the Lystra road, he had made him his closest friend. He was associated with him in his epistles, entrusted with important missions, taking the troublesome details of work off his hands in his care for all the churches. The childless old man loved him as a son, and he writes to the Philippians: "You know that as a son with his father he has been to me."

Now, in the lonely prison facing death, he wants to see Timothy again that he might give him final directions and advice and that his soul might bless him before he died.

Not that we are to imagine him sad and dispirited, thinking sentimentally of himself and his loneliness. Not a bit of it. Paul is not of that kind. The letter is full of hope and encouragement and wise advice for the guidance of the church in case Timothy should not arrive in time. But he greatly wants him to arrive in time. "I am longing to see you. If you would see me alive come soon. Do your diligence to come to me quickly—before the winter, if you can—before the end."

IX

Second Epistle to Timothy.

Paul, an apostle of Jesus Christ by the will of God, to Timothy my beloved son, grace, mercy and peace from God our Father and Christ Jesus our Lord.

I thank God whenever I make mention of you, as I do continually in my prayers, night and day. I am longing to see you that I may be filled with joy, remembering your tears when you parted from me. I remember your unfeigned faith, which dwelt first in your grandmother, Lois, and in your mother, Eunice, and I am persuaded also in you. Wherefore stir up the gift of God which is in you through the laying on of my hands.

Be not ashamed of the testimony of our Lord nor of me, His prisoner. . . . I am not ashamed, for I know Him whom I have believed, and I am persuaded that He is able to guard that which I have committed to Him against that day. Hold fast what you have heard from me in faith and love which is in Christ Jesus. That goodly treasure committed to your charge, guard through the Holy Ghost which dwelleth in us.

You know already that all those of Asia have deserted me. May the Lord grant mercy to the house of Onesiphorus, for he was not ashamed of my chain, but when he was in Rome he sought me diligently and found me. May the Lord grant him to find mercy in the Great Day.

Thou, therefore, my son, be strong in the grace which is in Christ Jesus. And the things which you have heard from me amongst many witnesses, the same commit to faithful men who shall be able to teach others also. . . .

Abide in the things which you have learned and been assured of, knowing of whom you have learned them, and that from a child you have known the Holy Scriptures which are able to make you wise unto salvation through faith which is in Christ Jesus. Every scripture given by inspiration of God is profitable for teaching, for reproof, for correction, for instruction in righteousness, that the man of God may be furnished completely unto every good work.

I charge thee in the sight of God and of Jesus Christ, who shall judge the quick and the dead at His appearing and His kingdom, preach the word, be instant in season and out of season, reprove, rebuke, exhort, with all long-suffering and teaching. . . .

Accomplish your ministry fully. For I am now ready to be offered up and the time of my departure has come. I have fought the good fight, I have finished my course, I have kept the faith. Henceforth there is laid up for me the crown of righteousness which the Lord will give me in that day.

Do your diligence to come to me shortly. Demas has forsaken me, Crescens and Titus I have sent on missions. Only Luke remains with me now. Bring Mark with you. Bring with you my cloak which I left with Carpus at Troas, and the books, especially the parchments. Do your diligence to come to me before winter. The Lord be with thy spirit. Grace be with you.

x

That is our last glimpse of Paul. Whether he ever got that old cloak and parchments, whether Timothy got to him in time we cannot tell. We hope for Paul's sake that it was so. They would have but a short time together anyway. For the end was now very close.

What a picture it would make, that final trial. The best man and the worst man in the world at the time facing each other. The Right and the Wrong meeting. And the Right was in the fetters and the Wrong was on the throne. It is often so in this topsy-turvy world. So often that, even apart from Revelation, men are constrained to believe in a great Setting-Right some day.

But even in this world things are not so topsy-turvy as they seem. For even here, in the long run, Right wins. Nay, even in the moment of seeming defeat Right wins. Who doubts which was happier that day—the brave old fighter who had lived his life for God and who, at its close, possessed of earthly goods just an old cloak and a few parchments, or the proud, wicked emperor, who had lived his life for self, who had exhausted life's enjoyments and dissipations and had boundless wealth and power at his disposal.

The trial was soon over. There was no advocate, no defender, no man stood by him. It mattered little. If Christians were accused of destroying Rome, and if

Paul was accused of being the Christian leader, what defence would avail in the state of public feeling at the time. The vote was for death. The prisoner was to be beheaded. Probably it was only his Roman citizenship that saved him from worse.

We have no details. There is a persistent tradition that, like his Master, he " suffered without the gate " at the Pyramid of Cestius on the Harbour Road.

We can easily picture the scene. The hot, white road, while the yelling mob, the small, quiet old man walking silently amid the guards with the light of another world in his eyes.

One hopes that they were men of the old Prætorian Guard who knew him and would shield him from the insults of that howling mob. Then the halt—the headsman's block—a broad sword flashing in the sunlight—and an old white head lying dishonoured on the ground. Not even the band of Christians, as in Stephen's day, " to make much lamentation over him."

The further scene it is not for us to paint when those eyes that closed thus in the darkness of death opened on ' a light that never was on sea or land,' and the poor humble soul who felt himself " the chief of sinners " was again with the Jesus of the Damascus road to give up the commission which he had received that day.

Doubtless, there were more glorious commissions for him now.

> We doubt not that for one so true
> God will have other nobler work to do

in the great adventure of the Hereafter. One day we shall know of that new adventure too. But not now. The curtain has fallen on Paul's earthly life. Suffice it that he has won his heart's desire, " to depart and be with Christ which is far better."

INDEX